D1236857

Original Music for Men's Voices:

A Selected Bibliography

by
WILLIAM TORTOLANO

The Scarecrow Press, Inc.
Metuchen, N. J.   1973

Library of Congress Cataloging in Publication Data

Tortolano, William.
  Original music for men's voices.

    1. Choral music—Bibliography. I. Title.
ML128.V7T66   016.784'1063   73-13930
ISBN 0-8108-0677-0

DEDICATED TO

Martha, Bill, Allegra, Jonathan

and

The Saint Michael's College Glee Club

past, present, future

ACKNOWLEDGMENTS

Professor Charles Fassett, Wheaton College, generously read the entire text in various stages of progress and offered valuable suggestions. Himself the editor of A Selected List of Choruses for Women's Voices, Professor Fassett gave of his time and encouragement. His kindness is greatly appreciated.

Dr. Henry Fairbanks, Saint Michael's College, very kindly read the entire text. In particular, he was most helpful in matters of style and in the organization of the Introduction. As always, Dr. Fairbanks is kind and most helpful.

Mr. Joseph Sullivan, assistant librarian, Saint Michael's College, helped research authors, titles and many other details. With his help, the college developed an interesting collection of recordings reflecting many compositions described in this book.

Dr. Marie Henault and the Rev. Richard Berube, S. S. E. , helped research many texts and were very kind.

Mrs. Leonard Pilus, faculty secretary at Saint Michael's College, typed and retyped the text many times. She was always most gracious and considerate. I cannot thank her enough for her patience and kindness.

CONTENTS

INTRODUCTION

"For many years it has been common to hear conductors of men's and women's choruses complain about the lack of a central bibliographical source to which they might turn for good material." This provocative challenge is so stated in J. Merrill Knapp's Selected List of Music for Men's Voices, published in 1952 by Princeton University Press. Now out of print, it also suffers from the persistent problem inherent in any such study: new material is being published and old titles are being withdrawn.

The task of finding original music for men's voices is often frustrating. There is much music of quality, but, unlike the availability of music for mixed voices, one must constantly seek out titles, composers, and publishers from a maze of information for the enterprising choral conductor. This is disseminated in a variety of publishers' catalogs, foreign and domestic; the collected works of composers; and many other sources. Considerable time, therefore, can be wasted in seeking quality music. To seek the significant, the distinctive and the aesthetic from the many titles available is always a challenge.

In addition to Professor Knapp's serviceable but out-of-print book, one can find useful lists from the publications of the American Choral Foundation. Recently, Professor Kenneth Roberts of Williams College has written A Checklist of Twentieth Century Choral Music for Male Voices. His titles are often fascinating, including works little known from Scandinavian composers. But a main problem is the unavailability of a large portion of these works. Moreover, many works listed are out of print. All this does not make the checklist any less valuable as musicological research. However, the chief need of the choral conductor is to find published, available music.

Similar problems of quality music and its availability are common to music for women's voices. Although there is a considerable body of composers and appealing texts for

7

both women's and men's voices alone, one must look harder
for it as the predominant part of the world's greatest choral
literature is largely for mixed voices. In the category of
music for women's voices A Selected List of Choruses for
Women's Voices by Arthur Locke and Charles Fassett (third,
revised edition, 1964, Smith College) is estimable. Somewhat more limited is Charles Burnsworth's Choral Music for
Women's Voices (Scarecrow Press, 1968). Both books, and
other studies, can give clues to possible material for men
by the use of the term "equal voices." Some compositions
lend themselves to both voicings.

A serious problem confronts the compiler of any
such lists. What should be included? A maze of entangling
questions unfolds. The first problem is to indicate those
works that are specifically written by the composer for adult
male voices. A second problem is to limit criteria to those
compositions that are not arrangements, folk or otherwise.
Boy sopranos, castrati, male altos and counter tenors present special problems. But, if one starts the search with
the premise of adult male voices, a large, exciting list can
be developed.

A great source for male voices is German Männerchor music written during the Romantic era. A profuse
number of scores poured from German music presses to
satisfy these needs, as this was a popular community and
parlor art. The pens of Mendelssohn, Brahms and, in
particular, Schubert and Schumann, were especially prolific.
Not all is of equal quality. Yet, for the sake of complete-
ness, this study has included available manifestations of the
era. The historically curious can find unusual texts and
instrumentation. Practically all are eminently singable.

Understandably, some of these works are of secondary
merit, but are historically of interest as well as revealing
of the facets of a composer's style. Even the "greats"
would often write simple, performable music of secondary
artistry in order to make a living or conform to prevailing
standards of the day.

Regretfully, much interesting material from Scandi-
navia is usually omitted. Some of it, by composers such
as Sibelius, is of real merit. However, a good segment is
untranslated and the language difficulties are extensive.
Much is out of print, or not normally available, except
through involved importation. American composers of this

era who received their training in Germany also wrote
music in this style.   However, many such pieces by Mac-
Dowell, Chadwick, Foote and Horatio Parker are no longer
in print.

Because many conductors are affiliated with liturgical churches, this study includes textual sources of practically all works so listed.   This makes their seasonal or
liturgical propriety clear and functional.   Besides, one can
assimilate programs of particular textual preferences.
"Anonymous" is here used for those texts that are quite
well known but have lost specific author-identity in history.
In particular, one finds this the case with medieval liturgical
texts of the Roman Catholic Church and Hebrew liturgy.   The
Roman Breviary and the Liber Usualis, often the source of
many texts, seldom specify an author.   Instead, a general
reference is given, such as "Medieval Text."   Texts in honor
of Mary are often difficult to identify.   "Unknown" refers to
the lack of information of any source whatsoever.

The Bible (particularly the Psalms) is the most popular source of textual inspiration.   Until quite recently
there has been a variation in numbering of the psalms for
Catholic and Protestant Bibles.   The latter is the usual
numeration (King James) followed in this study.   When the
Biblical title is given by the composer in Latin, an English
translation is usually provided.   The same is true of non-
Biblical sources.   Some French titles almost defy translations, such as the Poulenc works.   Debussy's "Invocation"
is a superb work, little known, by the great master of
Impressionism.   Schubert and other German Romanticists
are, in most cases, listed in the original and in English
translation--especially famous works like Schubert's
Widerspruch, or Contradiction.

Certain composers, like Bach, are available in several editions.   In such cases, a generally accepted musi-
cologically correct version is listed together with one or
two other possibilities.   In the case of Bach's Cantatas, the
Breitkopf und Härtel editions and the Henry Drinker editions
are listed.   An excellent source of information about the
Cantatas is Werner Neumann's Johann Sebastian Bach's Hand-
book of Cantatas, published in German by Breitkopf und Härtel.

Although "arrangements" of folk music are largely
excluded, it was felt that composers of the stature of
Bartók, Grieg, Stravinsky, Kodály, Poulenc, Copland,

Moussorgsky and Harris should be included. In these ex-
pressions, they went beyond ordinary arrangements in the
commercial sense and add an inherent style and contribution.
Bartók's use of folk melody, for example, is not merely
literal repetition of a tune, but a significant impregnation of
the composer's style. In a sense, the original melody is
almost recomposed through harmony and other techniques.

It could be a detailed study in itself to analyze the
"correct" spellings of different composers' names. One
recalls immediately Vittoria versus Victoria; Handl or Gallus.
It was decided to use the spelling that seemed prevalent by
most publishers. In this case it would be Vittoria and Handl
(not to be confused with Handel).

The up-dating of not only the Catholic Church but
many other Christian and Judaic denominations has replaced
many traditional texts. All of the Latin Masses included
(and there are many first-rate ones, including Harris,
Křenek, Langlais, Villa Lobos) utilize the traditional
Catholic text. A new English Mass text appeared in
1969, but so far few major talents have set it to music.
The almost mandatory inclusion of a congregational part
has so far not been of significant importance to the
great composers. Yet, it could be an interesting future
development.

The area of Mass settings for all voices (from 1903
when the Motu Proprio was written, to 1964 when the Second
Vatican Council promulgated its Constitution on the Liturgy)
is analyzed in detail in William Tortolano's doctoral disser-
tation: The Mass and the Twentieth Century Composer, University Microfilms, Ann Arbor, Michigan. The largely
undiscovered Psalms by Benedetto Marcello (50 of them)
offer a great potential in English translation for the liturgy.
These works are in a variety of vocal and instrumental
combinations, all quite functional for new liturgical innova-
tions, vernacularism and practicality.

The Broadway theatre, however expressive of the
American scene, must of necessity be largely excluded.
First, many octavos are pure arrangements; and secondly,
few are of high artistic quality. Their popularity bears
little relevance to valid inclusion with the works of a
Beethoven or Wagner. But there are some exceptions,
such as "The Fugue for Tinhorns" from Guys and Dolls.
Student songs from colleges have been essentially recomposed

by men like Orff and Johann Schein. They have, therefore, been included with this study.

The opera, in particular those by Verdi and Wagner, offers a truly marvelous storehouse of first-rate original male music. One can also find examples by Weber, Beethoven, Mozart, Rossini and others. Often, it is possible to delete a part, or parts, for women's voices, as it is common to find equal voice doublings. One such example is the "Chorus of Hunters" from Rossini's William Tell. The elimination of soprano and alto causes no noticeable loss. The general unavailability of Russian operas, including those by Glinka and Prokofiev, somewhat limits what is an exciting repertoire.

Although there might be a magnificent men's choral ensemble in some operas, they are difficult to extract from context. Berlioz presents such problems. Nevertheless, enterprising conductors could well study such works and it might be possible to extract large sections for concert purposes.

Specific ethnic connotations offer exciting repertoire enrichment. Folksong arrangements often clearly reflect a people's experiences or life style. Bartók and Kodály are great masters. Jewish composers are increasingly developing a modal style that offers innovative challenges. Samuel Adler, for example, has rich potential. Earlier Jewish composers such as Salomone Rossi or Lewandowski are not easily identifiable ethnically, except through the use of Hebrew texts. Gershon Ephros has contributed a useful collection: Cantorial Anthology.

A common complaint of conductors who direct choirs of limited vocal resources, is that there is a lack of "easy" unison or part music of quality: "Gebrauchmusik," as Hindemith called it. Suggested composers to research are Hindemith, Altenburg and Lou Harrison among many. Harrison's "Mass for Male and Female Voices" for trumpet, harp and strings (also called St. Anthony Mass) is based on authentic Indian melodies from Spanish Colonial California. It is a gem. It is possible to perform it with men only, but perhaps it loses much of its "color" and effect thereby. Yet, it is included because of its unusual texture and unique melodic genesis.

Although not specifically original for male chorus,

the Bach Cantatas contain rich possibilities.   Many of the
tenor-bass duets (soloists) are conducive to many voices.
The availability in English translations and the editorial
work of Henry S. Drinker make them recommendable.

Some composers issue the same works for both
mixed and equal voices.   Copland's opera The Tender Land
and Gretchaninoff's Russian anthems are such examples.
Mostly, music for mixed voices (though arranged for male
voices) is not given.   The exceptions are those composers
who specifically approve of arrangements or do their own
versions (e. g. Gretchaninoff).   In a few cases, where the
composition is so famous that it almost defies exclusion, it
was felt that reference should be made.

The availability of good music for choirs of limited
resources has always been a serious problem.   Most of the
great composers have not written simple music for such
groups.   It is possible, nevertheless, to discover in history
some exceptions, although not necessarily for equal voices.
Schubert's "German Mass in F Major" and the hymns of
Louis Bourgeois are only two such examples.   World Library
Publications have issued an extensive series of motets for
small Catholic choirs to be used on the various Sundays and
holidays of the liturgical year.   Although not all are excep-
tional, one can, through careful selection, find several interesting works; in particular, those by Richard Felciano and
Leo Sowerby.   Through Concordia Publishing House, Jan
Bender and Leo Kraft have produced a similar series for
Lutheranism.   It is important to add that their intention
was not strictly to be denominational.   Instead, one can
discern an ecumenical flowering.

Canada has a diverse heritage: English and French.
In addition, it has encouraged ethnic immigration since
World War II.   Both English and French schools are well
established.   Canadian composers of music for men's voices
are represented by the high artistic standard of Jean
Papineau-Couture, Healey Willan and Claude Champagne.

Black music, other than spirituals (of which there is
an enormous number of arrangements), is almost void of
works for men's voices.   Fela Sowande of Nigeria is an
exception, as is Ulysses Kay in the United States.   But they
do not show any ethnic borrowing except for the fact that
they are Black composers.   Black poet Langston Hughes is
used by Anthony Donato in his "Homesick Blues," as is

Paul Laurence Dunbar in Henry Cowell's "Day, Evening, Night, Morning."

The generally growing acceptance of serialism and electronic music is vastly neglected in choral literature. Future potential is evident in Richard Felciano's Pentecost sequence with electronic sounds. The Schönberg pieces are, of course, acknowledged serial masterpieces. Ernst Křenek's "Missa Duodecim Tonorum" is a unique setting of the Mass.

Some works have provocative titles or stories. One such example is Philip James' "General William Booth Enters Heaven." Booth was founder of the Salvation Army. This setting is highly evocative of their spiritual heritage and atmosphere. An enigmatic work is the Roy Harris "Mass for Male Voices and Organ." Rarely sung and now almost a curiosity item, it deserves hearing. The composer found himself at odds with ecclesiastical authorities at Saint Patrick's Cathedral by whom he was commissioned to write the work. In a New York Times interview he said that composers put a price tag on music. Highly offended, the authorities promptly withdrew the premiere. The entire event seems to have been unfortunately misunderstood. One of the most challenging works is Martinů's "Field Mass." Written as a memorial to Czech dead in World War II, it is scored for a large wind ensemble and voices. The instrumentation, however, is not available in piano reduction.

When a choral extract is taken from a large work, and is not available as an octavo, the piano-vocal score is listed as primary source. Often the entire choral parts are available. "L'Enfance du Christ" by Berlioz contains one particularly effective section for men's voices with bass solo. Although the men's chorus is not published separately, the entire choral parts are available.

In regard to practicality, those works that involve a large orchestra are here listed only as piano reductions if so available. "Rinaldo," by Brahms, would probably be performed more often with piano accompaniment than full symphonic instrumentation by most men's groups. However, such instrumentation is not listed. But it would be relatively easy to obtain it from the publisher. Although Stravinsky's "Oedipus Rex" demands a fairly large ensemble, in this case the instrumentation is given. As such, it is an integral part of the work and is rarely if ever done with piano alone.

The serious problem raised is what is "original" for
men's voices. One recognizes that vocal timbre has changed,
and that boys and men singing soprano and alto were intended
in former practice. Although boys are still an integral part
of Continental choirs, they are less common in the United
States. Rather than eliminate all the music that was written
with this voice disposition and, therefore, eliminate a rich
literature from contemporary usage, it was felt best to include this music (mainly Renaissance, and English of the
16th and 17th Centuries) in editions of equal voices for men.
The Italian, Casimiri, was particularly successful in editions
of Renaissance polyphony adapted in this combination.

Knapp says, "Some composers, when they used the
term 'ad aequales,' also expressly designated that the composition could be sung by either high or low voices as long as
they were equal. This meant by men an octave lower, if
the original notation was for high voices, or by women an
octave higher if the original was for low voices. While
this was apt to be true of the seventeenth century, it is by
no means always true of the sixteenth, and it is well known
that music which sounds well for women's voices often be-
comes muddy and thick when transposed 'down' an octave
for men. " Particularly adaptable to both scorings, the
Villa Lobos "Mass in Honor of Saint Sebastian" is quite
successful.

An attempt is made in this study to provide as complete as possible a listing of music available from commercial publishers in the United States or from European repre-
sentatives. These are accessible for purchase or in some
cases rental. Except for a few specialized cases, a list of
private publications or composer autographs is not included.
The reader is referred for help towards some interesting
material in this category by consulting the catalogs of
American Composers' Alliance or Composers' Autograph
Publications.

Besides titles, composers and their dates are included, together with scoring for voices, soloists, accompaniment, instruments, language, text source, publishers,
catalog numbers and other pertinent information. Collections such as Schubert's music are included as they are
fairly accessible in libraries and other central depositories.

First lines have been included when they differ from
the title. If only the title is given, the first line is the

same. Unless a foreign title is known exclusively in that
language (e.g., "Ave Maria"), an English translation has
been included. When the author or source of the text is
known, this information is included. In some cases, it is
difficult to trace a specific author because the author of the
text is lost in tradition. This is particularly true of medieval Catholic texts.

Except for music of great merit, tradition and fame,
art and solo song arrangements have been excluded. For
practical reasons, few examples before circa 1500 are included. This is one of the hazards of bibliographical
veracity. One must draw a line somewhere.

The reader is referred to the fortunate publications
recently of reproductions in small score of the complete
music of a composer. All of Schubert's music for male
voices is now available in four small score booklets at an
inexpensive cost from Edwin Kalmus.

Russian liturgical tradition offers beautiful selections,
largely for male chorus. Unfortunately, not much is available; but the persevering conductor can often find material
by writing or visiting Orthodox Churches. England has
produced a quantity of high quality of glees and choral music
for equal voices. Theirs is also the advantage of being in
English. But their suitability to equal voice choruses is
complicated by the fact that the English, particularly in
cathedral choirs, use almost exclusively boys for soprano.
The alto is sung by a male (counter tenor), or, less rarely,
boy-altos. When women sing this part, they are designated
contraltos.

This presents a difficult problem to those countries
where only adult males sing the parts. Unfortunately this
precludes use of much music in the United States by male
choruses, including works by Byrd, Purcell and other
English masters. When editions are published which are
designed for all adult male voices, these are included if
they are practical and incorporate musicological veracity.

Many Renaissance motets are designated "equal
voices": ad aequales or cum paribus vocibus. When clef
signs are clear, one encounters little difficulty in identifying
such as soprano, soprano-alto; alto; tenor, tenor-bass and
bass. These generally indicate some combinations of high
or low voices. One can also investigate the range. Some

writers claim that "chiavete" implies transposition. The
basis for inclusion has also been to some extent the actual
sound in performance and whether it is clearly articulate.
If a "muddy" sound results and lines are foggy, then this
can be considered a reason for not including the piece.
The clef does not per se indicate the voice part.

Useful references on texts and helpful interpretive
guidelines to choral music, expecially Bach Cantatas, can be
found in Henry Drinker's catalogs of the Drinker Choral
Library.   In addition, his Index and Concordance to the
English Texts of the Complete Choral Works of Bach, Bach
Chorale Texts with English Translations, and Melodic Index
and Texts of the Choral Works of Bach in English Translation are valuable.

No claim can be made herein to absolute compre-
hensiveness.   The question of whether a piece is an arrange-
ment or not has at times been difficult to determine.   Occa-
sionally, exceptions are made.   One such is "Simple Gifts, "
arranged by Irving Fine and used in Copland's ballet "Appa-
lachian Spring, " itself based upon a Shaker melody.

In Biblical references, (Arabic) numerals are designated for chapters or psalms (except where a composer
specifically does not do this) and verses.   Whenever possible, timings of compositions are given.   This information
was generally drawn from three sources: the duration of
the music as given by the composer or publisher (not a
usual practice); recordings; actual performances.   Although
duration may understandably vary from performance to
performance, an attempt has been made to give some
practical help, whenever possible.

The raison d'être of this volume is to present in
one place as complete a list as possible of music for men's
voices, with helpful references of stable value.   It should
aid a director in expanding his repertoire, thereby hopefully
saving many hours of frustrating research and fostering
some challenging programs.

ABBREVIATIONS OF TERMS

A.	alto
acc.	accompaniment
adap.	adapted
ad lib.	ad libitum [at pleasure]
anon.	anonymous
arr.	arranged
attr.	attributed
B.	bass
Bar.	baritone
bn.	bassoon
ca.	circa [about]
Cent.	century
cl.	clarinet
Col.	Colossians
comp.	compiled
cont.	continuo [figured bass]
Dan.	Daniel
div.	divisi [divided]
ea.	each
ed.	edited by, editor, edition
E. hn.	English horn
Eng.	English
ev.	equal voices
fl.	flute
Fr.	French
Ger.	German
H.	high
harm.	harmonized
Heb.	Hebrew
hn	French horn
HSD	Henry S. Drinker
Hung.	Hungarian
It.	Italian
L.	low
Lam.	Lamentations
Lat.	Latin
Matt.	Matthew
mvt.	movement

Norw.	Norwegian
ob.	oboe
op.	opus
opt.	optional
orch.	orchestra
org.	organ
perc.	percussion
pf.	pianoforte
Phil.	Philippians
picc.	piccolo
Port.	Portuguese
pts.	parts
pv.	piano-vocal score
Ps.	Psalm
S.	soprano
Sp.	Spanish
stb.	string bass
str.	strings
T.	tenor
timp.	timpani
trans.	translated
tromb.	trombone
unac.	unaccompanied
unis.	unison
va.	viola
vc.	violoncello
vers.	version
vn.	violin
vol.	volume
vs.	verse, verses

PUBLISHERS' ABBREVIATIONS AND ADDRESSES

AAC   Association of American Choruses, Drinker Choral Library, c/o The Free Library, Logan Square, Philadelphia, Pa. 19103

AB   Annie Bank, c/o WL

ABIN   Abingdon Press, 201 Eighth Ave., Nashville, Tenn. 37202

ACA   American Composers Alliance, 170 West 74th St., New York, N. Y. 10023

ALB   Alexander Broude, Inc., 1619 Broadway, New York, N. Y. 10019

AMP   Associated Music Publishers, c/o GS

AR   A-R Editions, Inc., 22 North Henry St., Madison, Wis. 53703

ARIS   Arista Music Co., Box 1596, Brooklyn, N. Y. 11201

ARP   Arrow Press, c/o BH

AUG   Augsburg Publishing House, 426 South Fifth Street, Minneapolis, Minn. 55416

BB   Bote and Bock, Berlin, c/o GS

BEL   Belwin-Mills Publishing Corp., Melville, N. Y. 11746

BH   Boosey and Hawkes Inc., Oceanside, N. Y. 11572

BHW   Breitkopf und Härtel, Wiesbaden, c/o GS

BLOCH   Bloch Publishing Co., 31 West 31st Street, New York, N. Y. 10001

19

BMC	Boston Music Company, 116 Boylston St., Boston, Mass. 02116
BMI-C	BMI Canada, Ltd., 41 Valleybrook Drive, Don Mills, Ontario, Canada. Also c/o AMP
BOU	Bourne, Inc., 136 W. 52nd St., New York, N.Y. 10019
BR	Brodt Music Co., P.O. Box 1207, Charlotte, N.C. 28201
BRBR	Broude Bros., 56 West 45th St., New York, N.Y. 10036
CAP	Composer's Autograph Publications, 1908 Perry Avenue, Redondo, Cal. 90278
CARY	Cary and Co., c/o GI
CF	Carl Fischer, Inc., 62 Cooper Square, New York, N.Y. 10003
CFP	C.F. Peters Corp., 373 Park Avenue, South, New York, N.Y. 10016
CHES	J. and W. Chester Ltd., Eagle Court, London ECIM 5 QD, England
CON	Concordia Publishing House, 3558 South Jefferson Avenue, St. Louis, Mo. 63118
CUR	Curwen, c/o GS
DC	Da Capo Press, 227 West 17th Street, New York, N.Y. 10011
DUR	Durand et Cie, c/o TP
EBM	Edward B. Marks Music Corp., 136 West 52nd Street, New York, N.Y. 10019
ECP	Editions Costellat, Paris, c/o MB
ECS	E.C. Schirmer, Inc., 112 South Street, Boston, Mass. 02111

EME	Editions Max Eschig, Paris, c/o AMP
EVC	Elkan-Vogel Co., Inc., c/o TP
FAB	Faber and Faber, c/o GS
FC	Franco Colombo, c/o BEL
FF	Fortesch Frères, c/o ECS
FMC	Frank Music Corp., 116 Boylston Street, Boston, Mass. 02116
GAL	Galaxy Music Corp., 2121 Broadway, New York, N.Y. 10023
GI	Gregorian Institute of America, 2115 West 63rd St., Chicago Ill. 60636
GP	Gregg Press, Westmead, Farenborough, Hants, England
GR	H.W. Gray Co., c/o BEL
GS	G. Schirmer, Inc., 609 Fifth Avenue, New York, N.Y. 10017
HEL	Hinrichsen Edition, Ltd., London, c/o CFP
HEU	Heugel et Cie, c/o TP
HF	Harold Flammer, c/o SP
HVS	Hanssler Verlag, Stuttgart, c/o CFP
IONE	Ione Press, c/o ECS
JB	Joseph Boonin, Inc., 831 Main St., Hackensack, N.J. 07601
JF	J. Fischer and Bro., c/o BEL
KAL	Edwin F. Kalmus, 1345 New York Avenue, New York, N.Y. 10019
L	Leeds Music Corp., c/o MCA

LC	Leukart Chorblatt, München, c/o AMP
LGGS	Lawson-Gould, c/o GS
MB	M. Baron Co., P.O. Box 149, Oyster Bay, N.Y. 11771
MCA	MCA Music Corp., 543 West 43rd Street, New York, N.Y. 10036
MCR	McLaughlin and Reilly Co., c/o Summy-Birchard Co., Evanston, Ill. 60204
MJQ	MJQ Music, Inc., 200 West 57th Street, New York, N.Y. 10019
MM	Mills Music Inc., c/o BEL
MMC	Mercury Music Corp., c/o TP
MP	Music Press, c/o TP
MRF	Musikverlag Rob Forberg, Bad Godesberg, Germany, c/o CFP
MRL	Music Rara, London, c/o TP
MSC	Music Sales Corp., 33 West 60th St., New York, N.Y. 10023
NOV	Novello, c/o BEL
OX	Oxford University Press, Inc., 200 Madison Avenue, New York, N.Y. 10016
RIC	Ricordi, c/o BEL
RK	Robert King Music Co., 7 Canton St., North Easton, Mass. 02356
ROW	Row Music Co., c/o CF
SAL	Salabert, 575 Madison Ave., New York, N.Y.
SB	Stainer and Bell, c/o GAL
SCH	Schott, c/o BEL

SIM   Simrock, c/o ECS

SMC   St. Michael's College, Fine Arts Dept., Winooski, Vt. 05404

SOU   Southern Music Co., (also Peer International Corp.), 1740 Broadway, New York, N.Y. 10019

SP   Shawnee Press, Inc., Delaware Water Gap, Pa. 19010

SZ   Suivini Zerboni, c/o MCA

TP   Theodore Presser Co., Bryn Mawr, Penn. 19010

UN   Universal Music, c/o TP

VLD   Verlag Ludwig Doblinger, Wien, c/o AMP

VRH   Van Rossum, Holland, c/o WL

WB   Warner Brothers Music, 1230 Avenue of the Americas, New York, N.Y. 10020

WIT   Witmark, c/o WB

WL   World Library Publications, 2145 Central Parkway, Cincinnati, Ohio 43214

WR   Winthrop Rogers Editions, c/o GS

INDIVIDUAL COMPOSERS

MIDDLE AGES

Of necessity, only a selected list of music from the
Middle Ages is included in this study. The general unavailability of performing editions, and difficulties in notation,
rhythm and style somewhat limit the inclusion of medieval
music by male choral groups. Nevertheless, some very
fine examples can be found, usually in collections of early
music. The following list is intended to help locate interesting sources of medieval music. Also included is a selected list of compositions from different historical periods
that make extensive quotes from Gregorian Chant.

Liber Usualis, Desclée Co., Tournai, Belgium.
Available in U.S. through GI or WL. This is the best
known, extensive collection of Gregorian Chant available.
The notation is in Gregorian and all the chants are in Latin.
All of them (hundreds) are for male (unison) voices.

A list of compositions using Gregorian melodies includes the following choral works (described in greater
detail in the catalog of compositions):

Binchois, A solis ortus cardine (chant in middle part).
Champagne, Ave Maria (chant used in all parts).
Duruflé, Messe cum Jubilo (based on Mass IX, cum
    jubilo, for feasts of the Blessed Virgin).
Langlais, Missa Salve Regina (extensive development
    in all parts).
Morales, Missa Ave Maria (development of the chant
    in all parts).
Surinach, Missions of San Antonio (four chants used
    in unison within orchestral texture).
Vittoria, Ave Maria (chant used in all parts).

Two works by Paul Creston, not described in the
catalog of compositions, are fine Gregorian inspired works:

25

(1) Mass of the Angels, unis., org., Eng., text: Mass,
JF #9711-10; and (2) Missa Adoro Te, unis. or 2 ev.,
org., Lat. text: Mass, JF #8751.

Collections of Medieval Music (non-Gregorian):
Adam de la Halle (1237-1287), Rondeaux à trois voix égales,
ed. Jacques Chailley; 16 titles: 3 ev., Fr., SAL (1:00-2:00
ea.). Renaissance to Baroque, 5 vols., ed. Lehman Engel;
vol. I: Quant Theseus, Guillaume de Machault (ca. 1300-
1377), SA (TB), unac.; Fr. text: Thomas Paien, Machault;
Eng. text: Marion Farquhar; vol. II: Per sequir la sperança,
Francesco Landino (ca. 1325-1397), TBB, unac.; It. text:
unknown; Eng. text: Farquhar; HF. Medieval to Renaissance
Choral Music, ed. Georgia Stevens, RSCJ, ev., unac. The
following items in the Stevens volume are from the Middle Ages:
(1) Anon., Polish., ca. 995, Hymn to St. Adalbert, unis.;
(2) Anon., Chartres, 11th Cent., Alleluia, Angelus Domini, 2
ev.; (3); Leoninus, Haec dies, 2 part organum, uses only two
words: Haec dies; (4) 13th Cent., Worcester Medieval Harmony,
Puellare gremium, 3 ev.; (5) 13th Cent., O Miranda Dei caritas,
3 ev.; (6) 13th Cent., Worcester Medieval Harmony:
Alleluia-Psallat, text: Ps. 15., 3 ev.; (7) Dufay: Flos
florium, 3 ev.; (8) Dunstable: Quam pulchra es, 3 ev.;
(9) Jacob Obrecht (1430-1505), Missa Sine Nomine, 3 ev.,
MCR #1158.

RENAISSANCE

1 AICHINGER, GREGOR (1564-1628). Assumpta est
  Maria (Sing to the Lord), arr. McKinney. unac.
  Lat. Text: Assumption, Second Vespers, Antiphon.
  Eng. Text: Howard McKinney. JF#7554. Also
  AB. (2:00)

2 ASOLA, GIAMMATEO (1560-1609). Hoc signum crucis,
  ed. Fouse. TTBB. unac. Lat. Text: Feast of the
  Holy Cross. (From 16 Liturgical works by Asola).
  A-R

3 ASOLA. Mass in the Eighth Mode (Missa Octavi Toni),
  ed. Lindusky. TTBB. unac. Eng. WL. Also: ed.
  Bank. AB

4 ASOLA. Mass Without a Name (Missa Sine Nomine).
  WL#EMO-1138-3

5 BOURGEOIS, LOUIS (ca. 1510-1561?). Two Evening
  Hymns: A Gladsome Light and Darkening Night, arr.
  C.F. Simkins, harm., Claude Goudimel. TTBB.
  unac. Texts: Greek, 3rd Cent. Eng. trans. Robert
  Bridges. OX #214

6 BRUMEL, ANTONE (1575-1620). Mater patris et filia,
  ed. Forbes. TBB. unac. Lat. Text: unknown.
  GS #11011. Also AB

7 BYRD, WILLIAM (1542-1623). Lord, in Thy Rage
  (Domine in furore); Songs of Sundrie Natures. TTB.
  unac. Eng. Text: Ps. 6. AMP #NYPM5. (2:00)

8 BYRD. Mass in Three Parts (Missa Sine Nomine), ed.
  Manzetti. TTB. unac. Lat. MCR #1385. Also AB.
  (20:30)

9 CAUSTON, THOMAS (-1569). Rejoice in the Lord,
  ed. H. Panteleoni. TTBB. unac. Eng. Text:
  Phil. 4: 4-7. CON #98-1534

10 CLEMENT, JACQUES (ca. 1510-1556?). [also known as
    Clemens non Papa]. Adoramus Te, ed. Davison.
    TTBB. unac. Lat. Text: asc. St. Francis of
    Assisi. ECS #948

11 CROCE, GIOVANNI (1557-1609). Ego sum pauper, ed.
    Rev. Walter Williams. TTBB. unac. Lat. Text:
    Ps. 69: 30, 31. Eng. Williams. ECS #698

12 DE BINCHOIS, GILLES (1400-1467). A solis ortus
    cardine, ed. Boepple. TTBB. unac. Lat. Text:
    Caelius Sedulius. MP. (1:00 x 4)

13 DEERING, RICHARD (-1630). Gaudent in caelis, ed.
    Turner. TT. org. Lat. Text: Magnificat, anti-
    phon, 2nd Vespers, Common of two or more Martyrs.
    AMC #437

14 DEERING. O bone Jesu, ed. Turner. TT. org. Lat.
    Text: trad. sacred. AMP #A437

15 DE SERMISY, CLAUDIN (1490-1562). Ceulx de Picardie
    (Picardy has Burghers), ed. Isabelle Cazeaux. TTBB.
    unac. Fr. Text: unknown. Eng. vers. Cazeaux.
    ALB #133-5. (0:30)

16 DE SERMISY. Lux aeterna (Eternal Light), ed. H. T.
    Luce. TTBB. unac. Lat. Eng. Text: Requiem
    Mass. BR #NC2

17 DES PREZ, JOSQUIN (1450-1521) [also known as des
    Pres]. Agnus Dei; Missa de Beata Virgine, ed.
    Boepple. TB. unac. MP #25. (1:10)

18 DES PREZ. Missa Mater Patris, ed. Forbes. TTBB.
    unac. Lat. (parody Mass based on Brumel motif
    of the same name). GS #2642. (Gloria is 6:00)

19 DES PREZ. Pleni sunt coeli; Missa Pange Lingua, ed.
    Boepple. TB. unac. Lat. MP #25

20 DES PREZ. Tu pauperum refugium, arr. WRS. TTBB.
    unac. Lat. Text: unknown. ECS #82

21 DUFAY, GUILLAUME (1400-1474). Gloria ad modum
    tubae, ed. Engel (in Renaissance to Baroque, Vol. 1).
    TB. 2 tromb. Lat. Text: Gloria; Mass Text. HF.
    (1:30)

22 DUFAY. Magnificat in the Eighth Mode, ed. Boepple.
    TB (and instruments). Lat. Text: Luke 1: 46-56.
    MMC #MC29. (5:00)

23 DUNSTABLE, JOHN (1370?-1453). Sancta Maria, ed.
    Bernard Rose. TBB. unac. Lat. Text: unknown.
    SB#5283

24 GABRIELI, GIOVANNI (1557-1612). Surrexit Christus,
    ed. Pantaleoni. TTB. org. or pf. Text: Lat.
    paraphrase of Luke 24:34. Eng. H. Pantaleoni.
    CON #97-6370

25 HANDL, JACOB (1550-1592) [also known as Jacobus Gal-
    lus]. Confirma hoc Deus (Confirm in Us, O Lord),
    ed. Martens. TTBB. unac. Lat. Eng. Text: Based
    on Ps. 67:29, 30, by Martens. CON #98-1655. Al-
    so AB.

26 HANDL. In nomine Jesu (In the Name of Jesus), ed.
    Walter Collins. TTBB. unac. Lat. Text: unknown.
    Eng. Collins. LG #51203. (1:00)

27 HANDL. Let the Voice of Praise Resound (Resonet in
    laudibus), ed. B. Rainbow. TTBB. unac. Text:
    Anon. Lat. Eng. vers. Rainbow. NOV #MV147

28 HANDL. O magnum mysterium, arr. McKinney. TTBB-
    TTBB. unac. Lat. Text: Responsory, Matins,
    Christmas; Paraphrase of Luke 2: 10-13. JF #7539.
    Also AB. (2:30)

29 HANDL. Regnum mundi; Opus Musicum Harmoniarum,
    ed. Boepple. TTBB. unac. Lat. Text: Non-Bibli-
    cal; Roman Breviary. MMC #MC32. Also AB.
    (1:00)

30 HANDL. Repleti sunt omnes, ed. Boepple. TTBB-
    TTBB. unac. Lat. Text: Acts 2: 4, 11. MMC
    #MC31. Also AB. (1:30)

31 HANDL. Trahe me post Te, ed. Boepple. TTBBB.
    unac. Lat. Text: Songs of Solomon I: 3, 2. MMC
    #MC32. (1:00)

32 HASSLER, HANS LEO (1564-1612). Cantate Domino,
    arr. Davison. TTBB. unac. Lat. Text: Ps.

96: 1-3.   ECS #68.   Also CON #98-341.   (2:00)

33   HASSLER.   Domine Deus, ed.   Swing.   TTBB.   unac.
Lat.   Eng.   Text: Ps.   96: 1-3; 11-13.   CON #98-
1341

34   HASSLER.   God Now Dwells Among Us (Verbum caro
factum est), ed.   Roger Wilhelm.   TBB.   pf.   or org.
Lat.   Eng.   Text: unknown.   Mark Foster Co. , Mar-
quette, Mich.   (2:00)

35   HASSLER.   Gratias agimus tibi, ed.   Peter Gram
Swing.   TTBB.   unac.   Lat.   Eng.   Text: Mass Text.
CON 98-1342 (out of print)

36   HASSLER.   Laetentur coeli, ed.   Swing.   TTBB.   unac.
Lat.   Eng.   Ps.   95: 11-13 (4 original male motets by
Hassler according to Swing: Laetentur caeli; Cantate
Domino: Domine Deus; Gratias agimus tibi).   CON
#98-1339.   Also NOV #136, ed.   B.   Rainbow

37   HENRY VIII, KING (1491-1547).   Quam pulchra es, ed.
Thurston Dart.   TTB.   unac.   Lat.   Text: Solomon,
7: 6, 7, 5, 4, 11, 12.   SB#5565

38   LASSUS, ORLANDUS (1530-1594) [also known as Orlando
di Lasso].   Cantiones duarum vocum (Magnum opus
1-XX), ed.   Boepple.   (12 Motets for 2 voices).
unac.   Lat.   MP.   (1:00-2:00 ea.)

39   LASSUS.   Hodie apparuit (On This Day), ed.   Maynard
Klein.   TTB.   unac.   Lat.   Eng.   Text: unknown.
GS #11783

40   LASSUS.   Three Psalms, ed.   Boepple.   TT(B)B.   unac.
Lat.   Eng.   (1) Psalm 25, Judica me, Domine; (2)
Psalm 5, Verba mea auribus; (3) Psalm 43, Deus,
auribus nostris.   Eng.   vers.   Harvey Officer.   MMC
#21.   (1:00 ea.)

41   LUYTHON, KAREL (1558-1620).   Missa Quodlibetica,
ed.   A.   Smijers.   TTBB.   unac.   Lat.   WL

42   MORALES, CHRISTOBAL DE (1500-1553).   Agnus Dei;
Missa L'Homme Armé, ed.   Leo Kraft.   TTB.   unac.
Lat.   Text: Mass.   MMC #MC 359.   (2:30)

43 MORALES. Missa Ave Maria, ed. E. Bruning. TTBB.
    unac. Lat. Text: Mass. WL.

44 MORLEY, THOMAS (1557-1603). I Go Before My
    Charmer, ed. G. W. Woodworth. TB(SA). unac.
    Eng. Text: Anon. ECS #824. (1:15)

45 MORLEY. Round, Around About a Wood, ed. Elliot
    Forbes. TTBB. unac. Eng. Text: Anon. GS
    #10745

46 MORLEY. Say, Dear, Will You Not Have Me?, ed.
    Forbes. TBB. unac. Eng. Text: Anon. GS
    #10746. (0:40)

47 NANINO, GIOVANNI (1545-1607). Hodie Christus natus
    est. TTBB. unac. Lat. Text: Christmas Day,
    Antiphon, Magnificat, 2nd Vespers. CF #2809

48 PALESTRINA, GIOVANNI DA (1524-1594). Assumpta
    est Maria, ed. Boepple. TTB. unac. (Instruments:
    str., winds or brass). Lat. Text: Antiphon, Ves-
    pers, Assumption. MMC #MC1. (4:25)

49 PALESTRINA. Ave Maria, arr. Harman. TTBB.
    unac. Lat. Text: Luke 1:28. HF. (3:00)

50 PALESTRINA. Benedictus; Mass; Repleatur Os Meum
    Laude, ed. Leo Kraft. TTBB. unac. Lat. Text:
    Mass. MMC #MC352 (3:00)

51 PALESTRINA. Supplicationes, ed. Woodworth. TTBB.
    unac. Lat. Text: Lamentations of Jeremiah. GS
    #9798

52 PONCE, JUAN (16th Cent.). Ave color vini clari, ed.
    Goodale. TTBB. unac. Lat. Eng. Text: student
    drinking song; The Court of Ferdinand and Isabella.
    GS #11082

53 PRAETORIUS, MICHAEL (1571-1621). In Peace and
    Joy (Mit Fried 'und Freud), ed. H. Pantaleoni. TTB.
    unac. Text: Ger. paraphrase of Nunc dimittis (Luke
    2: 29-32) by Martin Luther. Eng. Pantaleoni. CON
    #98-1715

54 RUFFO, VINCENZO (-1587). Adoramus Te, ed. Robert
    Hufstader. TTBB. unac. Eng. Text: asc. St.
    Francis of Assisi. MMC #MC78

55 SHEPHERD, JOHN (?-1563). Alleluia, confitemini (O
    Give Thanks), ed. Terry. TTBB. unac. Lat. Eng.
    Text: Ps. 135: 1. NOV #TM8

56 SHEPHERD. I Give You a New Commandment, ed.
    Watkins Shaw. A(T)TBB. org. ad lib. Eng. Text:
    John 13: 34-35. OX #18B

57 SHEPHERD. Magnificat and Nunc dimittis, ed. C. F.
    Simkins. ATTB. (possible to do Alto, 8ve. higher).
    unac. Eng. Text: Luke I: 46-56; Luke 2: 29-32.
    OX #45

58 TALLIS, THOMAS (1505-1585). Benedictus. TTBB.
    unac. Eng. Text: Scriptural adaptation. NOV # MT
    1536

59 TALLIS. Blessed Be the Lord, ed. Collins. TTBB.
    unac. org. ad lib. Eng. Text: Luke 1: 68-74. AMP
    #NYPM--30-6. (2:00)

60 TALLIS. If Ye Love Me, ed. Pantaleoni. TTBB.
    unac. Eng. Text: John 14: 14-17. CON #98-1520.
    (1:15)

61 TALLIS. O Lord, in Thee Is My Trust, ed. Pantale-
    oni. TTBB. unac. Eng. Text: unknown. CON
    #98-1684

62 TAVERNER, JOHN (1495-1545). Playnsong Mass for
    Four Men's Voices in the Dorian Mode, ed. Collins.
    TTBB. unac. Lat. CARY

63 TYE, CHRISTOPHER (1500-1573?). O Come Ye Servants
    of the Lord (Laudate nomen Domini), arr. John Hol-
    ler. TTBB. unac. Eng. Lat. Text: Ps. 134, free
    paraphrase. GR #1776. Also CON #98-1995

64 VITTORIA, TOMAS LUIS DA (1549-1611) [also known as
    Victoria]. Ave Maria, ed. Damrosch. TTBB. Lat.
    Text: Luke I:28. GS #6249. Also AMP; AB. (2:00)

65 VITTORIA. Jesu dulcis, ed. Davison. TTBB. unac.

Lat. Text: St. Bernard.   ECS #79

66 VITTORIA.   Judas, mercator pessimus, ed. D. Plott.
    TTBB.   unac. Lat. Text: unknown; possible Trope
    on Matt. 26:24.   BR #CD#3.   (1:30).   Also AB.

67 VITTORIA.   Lord, Do Thou Have Mercy (Miserere mei
    Domine), ed. B. Rainbow.   TTBB.   unac. Lat. Text:
    Ps. 6:3; Jeremiah 7:14.   Eng. trans. Rainbow.
    NOV #MV138

68 VITTORIA.   O sacrum convivum, ed.   Nicholas Temper-
    ley.   TTBB.   unac. Lat. Text: St. Thomas Aquinas.
    OX #A232.   (1:00)

69 VITTORIA.   O My God, I Am Not Worthy (Domine, non
    sum dignus), ed. Rainbow.   TTBB.   unac. Lat. Eng.
    Text: paraphrase of Matt. 8:8.   NOV #131

70 VITTORIA.   O vos omnes (O All Ye That Pass By), ed.
    Davison.   TTBB.   unac. Lat. Text: Lam. 1:12.
    ECS #915.   (3:30). Also ed. B. Rainbow.   Lat. Eng.
    NOV #137 (The alto part can be sung by 1st tenor one
    8ve higher).   (2:40)

71 WEELKES, THOMAS (ca. 1575-1623).   Let Thy Merciful
    Ears, O Lord, arr. S. Drummond Wolfe.   TTBB.
    unac. Eng. Text: Collect, X Sun. after Trinity, ac-
    cording to the Book of Common Prayer.   CON #98-
    1998

72 WEELKES.   Strike It up, Tabor.   TTB.   unac. Eng.
    Text: Anon. ECS #537.   (0:50)

73 WILBYE.   Weep O mine Eyes, ed. Noah Greenberg.
    TTB.   unac. Eng. Text: unknown.   AMP #NYPM3-
    1-6

BAROQUE

74 ALTENBURG, MICHAEL (1584-1640).   Drei Intraden (2
    for Advent, 1 for Christmas), ed. A. Egidi.   (1 and
    2) Nun Komm der Heiden Heiland.   (3) Wo Gott der

Herr nicht bei uns hält. unis. 3 vn. va. 2 vc. Ger.
Text: originally St. Ambrose, Veni redemptor gentium. CFP #HV-82

75 BACH, JOHANN SEBASTIAN (1685-1750). Cantata 4,
Christ Lag in Todesbanden: Mvt. 4, Jesus Christ
Our God's Own Son. T (unis.). 2 vn. cont. Text:
Eng. adap. HSD, after Luther. AAC. Also BHW.
Ger. (2:15)

76 BACH. Cantata 11, Lobet Gott in seinen Reichen: Mvt.
7, Recitative and Arioso, While Steadfastly They
Watched. TB. cont. Text: Eng. adap. HSD, after
Acts, I: 10-11. AAC. Also BHW. Ger.

77 BACH. Cantata 33, Allein zu Dir, Herr Jesu Christ:
Mvt. 5, Duet, God Whose Very Name Is Love. TB.
2 ob. org. cont. Text: Eng. adap. HSD, paraphrase of John 4:8 and Matt: 19: 19 (Ger. adap.
Johann Schneesing, 1541). AAC. Also BHW. Ger.

78 BACH. Cantata 36, Schwingt freudig euch empor: Mvt.
6, Chorale, Thou the Father of Us All. T (unis.)
2 E. hn. cont. Text: Paraphrase of Veni, Redemptor
Gentium (Nun komm, der Heiden Heiland) of St. Ambrose, by Luther. Eng. adap. HSD. AAC. Also
BHW. Ger.

79 BACH. Cantata 44, Sie werden euch in den Bann tun:
Mvt. 1, Duet, Out from Their Temples. TB. 2 ob.
bn. cont. Text: atr. Christian Weiss, paraphrase of
John 16:2. Eng. adap. HSD. AAC. Also BHW.
Ger.

80 BACH. Cantata 80, Ein feste Burg ist unser Gott:
Mvt. 5, Chorale, Tho Friends Appear. unis. 3 tr.
timp. 2 ob. d'amore. str. cont. Text: asc. Luther,
Eng. adap. HSD. AAC. Also BHW. Ger.

81 BACH. Cantata 125, Mit Fried und Freud ich fahr
dahin: Mvt. 4, Duet, Thruout the Whole Earth. TB.
2 vn. cont. Text: atr. Luther, after a free render-
ing of The Song of Simeon (Luke 2:29-32). Eng.
adap. HSD. AAC. Also BHW. Ger. (3:30)

82 BACH. Cantata 136, Erforsche mich, Gott: Mvt. 5,
Duet, We Suffer Sore, by Sin. TB. vn. (unis.).

cont. Text: Eng. adap. HSD. AAC. Also BHW. Ger.

83 BACH. Cantata 140, Wachet auf, ruft uns die Stimme:
Mvt. 4, Chorale, Zion Hears the Watchman Calling.
T (unis.). str. cont. Text: Matt. 25: 1-13. Eng.
adap. HSD. AAC. Also BHW. Ger. Fr. Eng.
(4:00)

84 BACH. Cantata 146, Wir müssen durch viel Trübsal:
Mvt. 7, Duet, O How Will I Glory. TB. 2 ob. str.
cont. Text: unknown. Eng. adap. HSD. AAC.
Also BHW. Ger.

85 BACH. Cantata 178, Wo Gott, der Herr, nicht bei uns
hält: Mvt. 4, Tenor chorale, They Who Would Brand
Me Heretic. T. (unis.). 2 ob. d'amore. cont.
Text: Justus Jonas. Eng. adap. HSD. AAC. Also
BHW. Ger.

86 BACH. Cantata 190, Singet dem Herrn ein neues Lied:
Mvt. 5, Duet, Jesus Is My All-in-All. TB. ob.
d'amore. cont. Text: Picander. Eng. adap. HSD.
Also BHW. Ger.

87 BACH. Cantata 196, Der Herr denket an uns (Wedding
Cantata): Mvt. 4, Duet, The Lord Prosper You.
TB. org. str. cont. Text: Ps. 115:14. Eng. adap.
HSD. AAC. Also BHW. Ger. Also: CFP #6079.
ed. A. Mendel

88 BACH. Easter Oratorio: Kommt, eilet und laufet.
Duet, TB. 3 tromb. 2 ob. str. cont. Text: Picander. KAL (3:15)

89 BUXTEHUDE, DIETRICH (1637-1707). Zion hört die
Wächter singen (Zion Hears the Watchman Singing),
ed. H. Clough-Leighter. TB. org. (pf.) Ger.
Text: Matt. 25: 1-13. trans. Katherine Winkworth.
ECS #538

90 CAVALLI, FRANCESCO (1602-1676). Three Hymns,
realized by Raymond Leppard. (1) Iste confessor.
TT. 2 vns. (2 va. ad lib.). cont. (2) Ave maris
stella and Deus tuorum militum. TTB. 2 vn. (2
va. ad lib.). cont. Text: Iste confessor, attr.
Rabanus Maurus. (3) Ave maris stella, str.

Fortunatus. Deus tuorum, Anon. 6th Cent. FAB.
(4:30 ea.)

91   CHARPENTIER, MARC ANTOINE (1634-1704). Laudate
     Dominum. TTB. org. Lat. Text: Ps. 148. WL

92   CHARPENTIER. Magnificat. TTB. 2 vn. vc. key-
     board. (original hautecontre, Tenor, Bass). Lat.
     Text: Luke 1:46-56. FF. (10:00)

93   ESTE, MICHAEL (1580-1648). How Merrily We Live,
     ed. H. Clough-Leighter. TTB. unac. Eng. Text:
     Anon. ECS #756. (2:00)

94   GIBBONS, ORLANDO (1583-1625). O Lord, Increase
     My Faith, arr. Howard Hinners. TTBB. unac.
     Eng. Text: unknown. GR#671

95   KINDERMANN, JOHANN (1616-1655). Creator Spirit,
     By Whose Aid, ed. Fritz Oberdoeffer. TB. 2
     vn. cont. Eng. Text: attr. Rhabanus Maurus.
     trans. John Dryden. CON #98-1482. (1:00 x3)

96   LOTTI, ANTONIO (1667-1740). Mass for Two Vocum
     Aequalium. TB. unac. Lat. Gloria, Kyrie, with
     Sanctus, Benedictus, Agnus Dei, by B. Cordans
     (1700-1757). AB

97   LOTTI. Mass for Three ev. TTB. unac. Lat. GI.
     Also AB.

98   LOTTI. Surely He Hath Borne Our Griefs (Vere lan-
     guores nostros), ed. Hunter. TTB. unac. Eng.
     Lat. Text: Isaiah 53: 4, 5. EBM #4458. Also
     ECS #70. (2:30)

99   MARCELLO, BENEDETTO (1686-1739). And With
     Songs I Will Celebrate, ed. Wienhorst. TB (SA).
     org. (pf.). Text: Ps. 13:6. Eng. adap. Stevens.
     CON #98-1047. (2:30)

100 MARCELLO. Oh, Hold Thou Me Up, ed. Wienhorst.
     TB (SA). org. Eng. Text: Ps. 17: 5, 6. adap.
     Stevens. CON #98-1046. (4:00)

101 MARCELLO. O Lord, Deliver Me, ed. Wienhorst.

TTBB. Text: Ps. 8: 1-2. Eng. adap. Stevens.
CON #98-1044. (2:00)

102 MARCELLO. Psalm X (TB); Psalm XIV (BB); Psalm
XXV (TB); Psalm XXII (TT); Psalm XLIII (B); and
Psalm XXX (TB) from Estro Poetico--Armonico
(50 psalms). The liturgy paraphrases were the
work of Girolamo Giustiniani. Originally published
at Venice between 1724 and 1726, this anthology
was also issued in an Eng. trans. edition by Avison
and Garth in 1757. GP: DC

103 MARTINI, GIOVANNI BATTISTA (1706-1784). In monte
oliveti, ed. Rev. Walter Williams. TTBB. unac.
Lat. Text: Matt. 26: 39, 41. Eng. Williams.
ECS #1234

104 MONTEVERDI, CLAUDIO (1567-1648). Angelus ad
pastores ait, ed. Boepple. 3 ev. unac. Lat. Text:
Luke 2: 10-11. (Christmas Day, Third Antiphon,
Lauds). MMC #24. (1:00)

105 MONTEVERDI. Hodie Christus natus est, ed. Boepple. 3 ev. unac. Lat. Text: Christmas Day, Antiphon, Magnificat. MMC #24. Also FC #NY2041.
(1:30)

106 MONTEVERDI. Lauda sion Salvatorem (Praise the
King of Heaven), ed. Vene. TTBB. unac. Text:
Lat. St. Thomas Aquinas. Eng. Heiberg. FC#NY2031

107 MONTEVERDI. Veni, sponsa Christi (Come, Thou
Faithful Servant), ed. Vene. TTB. unac. Lat.
Eng. Text: Matt. 25: 34. RIC #NY 20332

108 PEPUSCH, JOHN (1667-1752). Fill Every Glass; The
Beggar's Opera. TB. pf. T. solo. Text: John
Gay. BH #1403. (1:15)

109 PEPUSCH. Let Us Take the Road; The Beggar's
Opera. arr. Austin. TTBB. pf. T. solo. Eng.
Text: John Gay. BH #1403. (1:15)

110 PITONI, GIUSEPPE (1657-1743). Cantate Domino (O
Sing Ye To The Lord), ed. Norman Greyson.
TTBB. unac. Lat. Eng. Text: Ps. 95. BOU
#ES56.

111 PITONI. Missa in Nativitatae. TTBB. unac. Lat.
     CHES.

112 PURCELL, HENRY (1659-1695). O, I'm Sick of Life,
     cont. realized Arnold Goldsborough. TTBB. org.
     Eng. Text: George Sandys. NOV #PSR 13.

113 PURCELL. Plung'd in the Confines of Despair, ed.
     Franklin Zimmerman. TTB. cont. Eng. Text:
     Ps. 130, paraphrase. SP C195

114 PURCELL. Sound the Trumpet. TB(SA). pf. Eng.
     Dutch. Text: unknown. Ed. Musico, The Hague,
     c/o WL. (0:45)

115 PURCELL. The Three Fairies, ed. H. Clough-Leight-
     er. TTB. unac. Eng. Text: Anon. ECS #535

116 ROSENMULLER, JOHANN (1620-1684). Since the World
     Is Only Passing, ed. Richard Peek. unis. pf. Eng.
     Text: unknown. CON #98-1820

117 SCHEIN, JOHANN (1586-1630). From Depths of Woe I
     Cry to Thee; Opella Nova. 2 ev. (TT). pf. Eng.
     Text: Luther. CON #98-1860

118 SCHEIN. O Lord, Look Down from Heaven; Opella
     Nova. TT. pf. Eng. Text: Luther. CON #98-
     1860

119 SCHEIN. Studentenschmauss (Two Student Songs from
     the University of Leipzig), arr. 5 parts, Forbes.
     TTBB. unac. Ger. GS #1057

120 SCHUTZ, HEINRICH (1585-1672). Attendite, popule
     meus, legem meum. B solo. (unis. chorus).
     4 tromb. cont. Text: unknown. MRL

121 SCHUTZ. Give Ear, Oh Lord (Erhöre Mich); Sacred
     Concert (Bk. I, no. 8), ed. Paul Boepple. TT.
     org. Ger. Text: Ps. 4:1; Ps. 5:2. MMC #MC13.
     (1:45)

122 SCHUTZ. Great Is Our Lord (Der Herr ist gross);
     Sacred Concert (Bk. I, no. 5), ed. Boepple. TT.
     org. Eng. Ger. Text: Ps. 145: 3-4. Eng. Harvey
     Officer. MMC #MC17. (2:30)

123 SCHUTZ. O Mighty God, Our Lord (O lieber Herre
    Gott); Sacred Concert (Bk. I, no. 6), ed. Paul
    Boepple. TT. org. Eng. Ger. Text: Johann
    Spanenburg. MMC #MC18. (3:10)

124 SCHUTZ. Why Afflict Thyself, O My Spirit (Was be-
    trübst du dich, meine Seele); Sacred Concert (Bk.
    II, no. 13), ed. Paul Boepple. TT (SS). cont.
    Various instruments possible (vn. ob. or fl. vc. stb.
    bn. ad lib.). Eng. Ger. Text: Ps. 42:11. MMC
    #MC20. (4:45)

125 SCHUTZ. Christmas Story: High Priests and Scribes,
    ed. Arthur Mendel. BBBB. org. (pf.) or 2 tromb.
    Ger. Eng. Text: Matt. 2: 5, 6. GS. (2:45)

126 SCHUTZ. Christmas Story: The Wise Men From the
    East. TTT. org. (pf.) 2 vn. and bn. Eng. Ger.
    Text: Matt. 2: 2. GS. (2:15)

127 SCHUTZ. One Thing Have I Desired (Eins bitte ich
    vom Herren); Kleine geistliche Konzert; ed. Ulrich
    Leupold. TT. org. Eng. Ger. Text: Ps. 27:4.
    CON #98-1369

128 SEELE, THOMAS (1599-1663). Benedicam Dominum.
    TTBB. cont. Lat. Text: Ps. 33: 2-3. HVS
    #Fh-1, 349.

129 SEELE. Confitemini Domino. TTBB. cont. Lat.
    Text: Ps. 104: 1-3. HVS #FH-1, 348

130 SEELE. In me transierunt. TTBB. cont. Lat. Text:
    Ps. 87:17; 37:11, 18, 22. HVS #FH-1, 342

131 SEELE. Si bona suscepimus. TTBB. cont. Lat.
    Text: Job 2:10; 1:21. HVS #FH-1, 347

132 TOMKINS, THOMAS (1572-1656). The Heavens Declare
    the Glory of God, ed. Stevens. TTBB. unac. Eng.
    Text: Ps. 19: 1-4. CON #98-1432

133 TOMKINS. O How Amiable Are Thy Dwellings, ed.
    Maurice Bevan. ATT(B)B (can be done TTBB).
    opt. org. Eng. Text: Ps. 84: 1, 2. OX #38

CLASSICAL PERIOD

134 BEETHOVEN, LUDWIG VAN (1770-1827). O welche
     Lust; Fidelio, ed. Rhodes. TTBB. pf. T. B.
     solos. Ger. Text: Schikaneder. Eng. trans. W.
     Rhodes. CF #CM2245. Also GS #1169. (3:30)

135 BEETHOVEN. Song of Farewell. TT (B) B. unac.
     Text: Ger. Jos. Ritter van Seyfried. Eng. trans.
     and adap. HSD. AAC.

136 BEETHOVEN. William Tell: Song of the Monks (Swift
     in Its Course Comes Death to Man). TBB. unac.
     Text: Ger. Schiller. Eng. trans. and adap. HSD.
     AAC #28

137 COCCHI, GIOACCHINO (1715-1804). Colla bottiglia in
     mano, ed. David Randolph. TBB. unac. It. Text:
     unknown. LGGS

138 HAYDN, FRANZ JOSEPH (1732-1809). Dreistimmige
     Gesänge (Three-Part Songs). TTB. pf. Ger.
     (1) An die Frauen. Text: Second Ode of Anacreon,
     trans. G. A. Bürger. (2) Daphnens einziger Feh-
     ler. Text: Anon. CFP #4936.

139 HAYDN. Maiden Fair, O Deign To Tell. Eng. vers.
     Thomas Oliphant. TTB. pf. Text: Oliphant.
     GR#527

140 MOZART, WOLFGANG AMADEUS (1756-1791). Die
     Maurerfreuden, KV 471. TTB. T. solo. pf. Ger.
     Text: Franz Petran. BHW #5929

141 MOZART. Dir, Seele des Weltalls, KV 429. TTB.
     S. solo. pf. Ger. Text: unknown. BHW #429

142 MOZART. Eine kleine Freimaurerkantate, KV 623.
     TTB. TB solos. pf. Ger. Text: Em. Schikaneder.
     BHW #5930

143 MOZART. Zwei Prater-Kannons (Two Canons). 4 ev.
     unac. Ger. Text. Mozart. VLD

144 MOZART. Magic Flute: Three choruses (O Isis,
     Schenket der Weisheit Geist; Bewahret Euch; O Isis,

Welche Wonne). TTBB. B. solo. pf. Text: Eng.
Cleveland Jauch. Ger. E. Schikaneder and Gieseke.
HF. (3:00 ea.)

145 MOZART. Idomeneo: Pietà, numi pietà, (Act I).
TTBB-TTBB. pf. It. Text: Giammatteo Varesco.
Publishers: International Music Co.

ROMANTIC ERA

146 BELLINI, GAETANO (1801-1835). Norma: Coro di
guerrieri (Non parti? Finora e al campo), Act
II, sc. 4. TTB. pf. It. Also, sc. 5 is possible:
TTB. B. solo. Text: Felice Romani. RIC.
(4:00)

147 BERLIOZ, HECTOR (1803-1869). Le Chant des Bre-
tons, ed. Kunzel. TTBB. pf. Fr. Eng. Text:
Julian A. P. Brizeaux. BH #5401

148 BERLIOZ. Choruses from The Damnation of Faust.
(Soldiers Chorus and Students Chorus). Voice parts
modified and arr. by Clough-Leighter. TTBB. pf.
Ger. Text: Goethe. Eng. trans. Henry Chorley.
ECS #565. Also: two other sections; Sc. VI,
Choeur de Buveurs (Oh, qu'il fait bon) and Fugue,
Sur le Thème de Brander--Amen.

149 BERLIOZ. L'Enfance du Christ; Chorus of Magicians,
Part I, scene IV. TTBB. pf. B. solo. Fr. Text:
Berlioz. Eng. John Bernhoff. GS. (4:15)

150 BERLIOZ. Requiem. Lat. Text: Requiem Mass.
GS. (1) Quid sum miser. TTB. (3:15); (2) Hosti-
as. TTBB. (3:00); (3) Agnus Dei. TTBB. (4:00)

151 BERLIOZ. Serenade of the Capulets (Ohé, Capulets,
Bonsoir); Romeo and Juliet, op. 17. TBB-TBB.
pf. Fr. Text: E. Deschamps. Eng. trans. John
Bernhoff. KAL (1:15)

152 BIZET, GEORGES (1838-1875). Carmen: Act I, Sur
la Place. TB. B. solo. Fr. Text: Meilhac and
Halevy. GS. (2:00)

153 BLOW, LEO (1878-?). Shivisi, op. 4. TTBB. unac.
    Heb. (from Cantorial Anthology. Vol. 4, ed.
    Ephros). Text: Hebrew Liturgy. BLOCH

154 BRAHMS, JOHANNES (1833-1897). Alto Rhapsody.
    TTBB. org. A. solo. Text: Goethe, Harzreise
    im Winter. Eng. trans. John Moment. JF #8559.
    (10:00)

155 BRAHMS. Five Songs for Male Chorus (Fünf Soldaten-
    lieder), op., 41, ed. Leonard de Paur. TTB.
    unac. Ger. Text: Carl Lemcke. Eng. Text: de
    Paur. (1) My Horn Shall Sound in Trouble's Vale
    (Ich schwing mein Horn); (2) All Volunteers Come
    (Freiwillige her!); (3) The Last Escort (Geleit);
    (4) Marching (Marschieren); (5) Take Care (Gebt
    acht). LGGS #51450. (17:00)

156 BRAHMS. Liebeslieder Waltzer, op. 52 (Love Waltzes),
    ed. Shaw. pf. 4 hands. Ger. Eng. Suitable for
    chorus: (3) O die Frauen, TB, (1:15). (14) Sieh,
    wie ist die Welle klar, TB, (1:15). (17) Nicht-
    wandle, T, (2:15). Text: Georg Friedrich Daum-
    er. LGGS #834

157 BRAHMS. Neue Liebeslieder Waltzer, op. 65. pf.
    4 hands. Ger. Following suitable for chorus: (No.
    4) Ihr schwarzen Augen. (B); (0:50). (No. 10)
    Ich kose süss (T); (0:50). Text: Georg Friedrich
    Daumer. Eng. Natalia Mac Farren. SIM

158 BRAHMS. Rinaldo, op. 50. TTBB. pf. Bar. solo.
    Text: Goethe. Eng. trans. HSD. AAC #10

159 BRUCKNER, ANTON (1824-1896). Ave Maria. TTBB-
    TTBB. unac. Lat. Text: Luke 1:28. ARIS
    #AE112 (3:45)

160 BRUCKNER. Fest-Cantate, ed. Karl Etti. TTBB.
    orch. reduced for pf. Ger. Text: Max Prammers-
    berger. VLD

161 BRUCKNER. Inveni david. TTBB. 4 tromb. ad lib.
    Lat. Text: Ps. 89: 20-21. (Gradual, Mass. of a
    Martyr--Bishop). CFP #6318

162 BRUCKNER. Locus iste, ed. Linshinsky. TTBB.

unac. Lat. Text: Gradual, Dedication of a Church.
ARIS. #AE155

163 BRUCKNER. The Noblest of Songs (Das deutsche lied),
ed. J. Park. TTBB. pf. Eng. Ger. Text: Erich
Fels. BR. #VF2. (3:00)

164 BRUCKNER. Trösterin Musik. TTBB. unac. Ger.
Text: A. Seuffert. UN #UE3299. (4:00)

165 BRUCKNER. Um Mitternacht. TTBB. unac. Ger.
Text: unknown. UN #UE3292. (5:00)

166 CHERUBINI, LUIGI (1760-1842). Requiem in D Minor.
TTB. orch. score reduced for pf. Lat. CFP #51.
(45:00)

167 CORNELIUS, PETER (1824-1874). Requiem aeternam
(Calm Repose Eternal), ed. Clifford G. Richter.
TTBB. unac. Lat. Eng. Text: Requiem Mass.
ALB #814-5. (2:15)

168 DONIZETTI, GAETANO (1797-1848). The Soldier's
Chorus; The Daughter of the Regiment, (Act I),
adap. S. Northcote. TTBB. pf. Eng. Text: Ed.
Miller. RIC #LD 472. (1:45)

169 DONIZETTI. Lucia di Lamermoor: Percorriamo le
spiagge vicine, Act I, sc. I. (based on the Walter
Scott novel). TBB. T. solo. pf. It. Text: Salva-
tore Cammarano. GS. (3:00)

170 DVORAK, ANTONIN (1841-1904). Gram (Grief); 3
Slovak Men's Songs, op. 43, ed. Woodworth.
TTBB. pf. 4 hands. Eng. Text: Ger. Th.
Cürsch-Bühren. GS #9813

171 DVORAK. Mägdlein im Walde (Maiden in the World);
3 Slovak Men's Songs, ed. Woodworth. op. 43.
TTBB. pf. 4 hands. Eng. Text: Ger. Cürsch-
Bühren. GS #9812. (Only 2 songs from op. 43
are published)

172 DVORAK. Stabat Mater op. 58: Fac me vere tecum
flere, sc. VI. TTBB. T. solo. orch. reduced for
pf. Lat. KAL #6162. Also NOV. Eng.

173 GERICKE, WILHELM (1845-1925). The Autumn Sea,
    op. 8, no. 3. TTBB. unac. Text: Eng. vers.
    Dr. Th. Baker. BMC #134

174 GERICKE. Chorus of Homage. TTBB. pf. Eng.
    Text: Eng. vers. Louis C. Elson. BMC #859

175 GOUNOD, CHARLES (1818-1893). Soldiers' Chorus;
    Faust. TTBB. pf. Eng. Text: Barbier and
    Carré. GS #4283. Also TP #312-20196.

176 GRIEG, EDVARD (1843-1907). Album for Male Voices,
    op. 8, no. 30. (8 choruses based on Norwegian
    Folk, including Grieg's favorite: The Great White
    Host). TTBB. Bar. solo. unac. Text: Eng.
    trans. Percy Grainger. CFP #2492

177 GRIEG. Länderkennung (Recognition of the Land), op.
    31. TTBB. pf. Bar. solo. Eng. Fr. Ger. Norw.
    Text: Björnstjerne Björnson. CFP #2085. (7:00).
    Also GS #1013. Eng. Ger.

178 GRIEG. Zwei Gesänge aus, Sigurd Jorsalfar, op. 22.
    TTBB. Bar. solo. pf. Ger. Text: Björnson.
    CFP #2660

179 HENSCHEL, GEORG (1850-1934). Morning Hymn, op.
    46., no. 4. TTBB. pf. Ger. Text: Robert
    Reinick, Eng. trans. Dirk van der Stucken.
    CF#CM 2126. (2:00) Also BMC #2133

180 LEWANDOWSKI, LOUIS (1821-1894). Ase L'Maan
    (from Cantorial Anthology Vol. I), ed. Ephros.
    TTBB. unac. Heb. Text: Jewish Liturgical.
    BLOCH

181 LEWANDOWSKI. V'al Y'de Avodecho, no. 2 (from
    Cantorial Anthology, Vol. I), ed. Ephros. TTBB.
    unac. Heb. Text: Jewish Liturgical. BLOCH

182 LISZT, FRANZ (1811-1886). Gaudeamus igitur--Hu-
    moreske, ed. Erich Kunzel. TTBB. pf. Lat.
    Text: trad. Ger. BH #5408

183 LISZT. Requiem Mass for Male Voices: Requiem
    (9:00); Dies irae (15:00); Offertorium (7:30); Sanctus
    (8:30); Agnus Dei (5:30); Libera (5:00). (Tot.
    51:00). TTBB. org. Lat. c/o JB

184 MENDELSSOHN, FELIX (1809-1847). Antigone, op.
55. TTBB-TTBB. pf. Eng. Text: W. Bartholomew., after Sophocles. NOV. Also JB #492

185 MENDELSSOHN. Der Jäger Abschied (The Hunter's
Farewell), ed. Clough-Leighter. TTBB. unac.
Ger. Eng. Text: Josef von Eichendorff. ECS
#559. Also GS #4992; Eng. vers. Clarence Alvord.

186 MENDELSSOHN. Festgesang an die Künstler (Festival
Ode), op. 68. TTBB-TTBB (solo quartet). Brass
(4 hns. 4 tr. 3 tromb. Bar. tuba). Ger. Text:
Schiller. Eng. trans. Robert A. Hall, Jr. RK
#615. Also JB #1210. (7:30)

187 MENDELSSOHN. Lieder fur Männerstimmen (Songs
for Men's Voices). All in Ger. (Titles not listed
in Index of first lines and titles). (1) Türkisches
Schenkenlied, op. 50., no. 1. TTB. unac. Text:
Goethe. (2) Der Jäger Abschied, op. 50, no. 2.
TTBB. 4 hns., tromb. Text: Eichendorff. (3)
Sommerlied, op. 50, no. 3. TTBB (Soli)--TTBB.
unac. Text: Goethe. (4) Wasserfahrt, op. 50, no.
4. TTBB. unac. Text: Heine. (5) Liebe und
Wein, op. 50, no. 5. TTBB. B solo. unac.
Text: unknown. (6) Wanderlied, op. 50, no. 6.
TTBB (Soli)--TTBB. unac. Text: Eichendorff.
(7) Der Frohe Wandersmann, op. 75, no. 1. TTBB.
unac. Text: Eichendorff. (8) Abendständchen, op.
75, no. 3. TTB. unac. Text: Goethe. (9)
Trinklied, op. 75, no. 3. TTB. unac. Text:
Goethe. (10) Das Lied vom Braven Mann, op. 76,
no. 1. TTBB. B. solo. unac. Text: Heine.
(11) Comitat, op. 76, no. 4. TTBB. unac. Text:
H. Fallersleben. (12) Beati mortui, op. 115, no.
1. TTBB. unac. Lat. Text: Apocalypse 14:13.
(13) Periti autem, op. 115, no. 2. TTBB. unac.
Lat. Eng. Text: Dan. 12:3, 4, and Matt. 3:43.
(14) Jaglied, op. 121, no. 1. TTBB. (soli)-TTBB.
unac. Text: Scott. (15) Im Süden, op. 120, no. 2.
TTBB. unac. Text: unknown. (16) Zigeunerlied,
op. 120, no. 4. TTBB. unac. Text: Goethe.
(17) Ersatz für Unbestand. TTBB. (soli)-TTBB.
unac. Text: Rückert. CFP 1772

188 MENDELSSOHN. The Righteous Living Forever (Periti
autem), op. 115, no. 2. TTBB. pf. Lat. Eng.

Text: adap. from Dan. 12: 3, 4, and Matt. 13:43.
NOV #255. (2:00). Also CF.

189 MENDELSSOHN. Say, Where Is He That Is Born King
of Judah; Christus. TBB. org. Eng. Text: adap.
Glasser. from Matt. 2:2. ECS #1611

190 MOUSSORGSKY, MODESTE (1839-1881). Four Russian
Love Songs. TTBB. unac. T. solo in #1. 2T.
solos in #4. Text: Eng. Roger Maren. EBM #54

191 MOUSSORGSKY. Khovanstchina: Act II, Sc. I, L'Here-
sie and Act III, Sc. VI, Ah, nul chagrin. TTB.
pf. Fr. Eng. vers. Rosa Newmarch. Publishers:
Breitkopf und Härtel.

192 OFFENBACH, JACQUES (1819-1880). La Belle Hélène:
Bacchanale. TTB. pf. Fr. Text: Meilhac and
Halevy. GS#9799. (2:00)

193 OFFENBACH. Tales of Hoffmann: Drig, Drig, Drig
and Il était une fois. TTB. pf. Fr. Text: Bar-
bier. KAL #6363. (2:30)

194 RIMSKY-KORSAKOV, NICOLAI (1855-1908). Chorus of
Warriors; The Legend of Kitezh, ed. Fitzgerald.
TTBB. pf. Text: Eng. vers. Bernard Fitzgerald.
FC #NY1478

195 ROSSINI, GIOCCHINO (1792-1868). William Tell: Coro
di cacciatori i di svizzeri (Chorus of Hunters and
Swiss), Act II. TTBB. pf. B. solo. It. Hunter's
Chorus, men only; Swiss chorus include S. and A.
parts which can be deleted. Text: based on Schiller novel. BH

196 ROSSINI. Chant Funèbre, ed. Kurt Stone (composed in
1864 upon the death of Giacomo Meyerbeer). TTBB.
T. drum. Fr. Eng. Text: Anon. JB #103 (4:00)

197 ROSSINI. Mille grazie, mio signore: Barber of Se-
ville. TTB. T. B. solos. pf. It. Eng. Text:
Cesare Sterbini. GS

198 SCHUBERT, FRANZ (1797-1828). Die Nacht (The
Night), op. 17, no. 4, ed. James Erb. TTBB.
unac. Text: Ger. F. A. Krummacher. Eng.
Alice Parker. LGGS. #786. (2:30)

199 SCHUBERT. Der Gondelfahrer (In the Gondola), op.
28. TTBB. pf. Text: Ger. Mayrhofer. Eng.
trans. HSD. AAC #103. Also LGGS #512

200 SCHUBERT. Geist der Liebe (Spirit of Lovers), op.
11, no. 3, ed. Erb. TTBB. pf. Ger. Eng. Text:
Matthisson. GS#774. (2:30)

201 SCHUBERT. Grab und Mond (The Grave and the
Moon), ed. Donald Plott. TTBB. unac. Ger.
Text: J. G. Seidl. Eng. Howard French. BR
#DC1

202 SCHUBERT. La Pastorella (The Shepherdess), ed.
Shaw-Parker. TTBB. pf. It. Text: Goldoni.
Eng. Alice Parker. LGGS #512.

203 SCHUBERT. Nachtgesang im Walde (Night Song in the
Forest), op. 139b, ed. Jan Meyerowitz. TTBB.
4 hns. Ger. Text: J. G. Seidl. Eng. Peter John
Stephens. BRBR #140. (6:00)

204 SCHUBERT. Salve Regina. TTBB. unac. Text: attr.
Herman Contractus. AAC #102

205 SCHUBERT. Song of the Spirits Over the Water (Gesang der Geister über den Wassern), op. 167. Revised, Herbert Zipper. TTTTBBBB. pf. (string
parts on rental: 2 va. 2 vc. stb.) Ger. Text:
Goethe. Eng. Roger Maren. EBM #41. Also
AAC #204. Eng. Text: HSD. (10:00)

206 SCHUBERT. Ständchen (Serenade), op. 135, ed. Shaw.
TTBB. A. solo. pf. Ger. Eng. Text: Franz
Grillparzer. GS #521. (5:30)

207 SCHUBERT. Widerspruch (Contradiction), op. 105, no.
1, ed. Shaw-Parker. Ger. Text: J. G. Seidl.
Eng. Alice Parker. LGGS #513

208 SCHUMANN, ROBERT (1810-1856). Blaue Augen hat
das Mädchen, op. 138, no. 9. TB. pf. Ger.
Text: Geibel. (from the Spanischen Liebes-Liedern).
CFP #2392

209 SCHUMANN. Drei Lieder für Männerchor, op. 62.
TTBB. unac. Ger. (1) Der Eidgenossen

Nachtwache. Text: J. von Eichendorf. (2) Frei-
heitslied. Text: F. Rückert. (3) Schlachtgesang.
Text: F. G. Klopstock. CFP #EP 2527B

210 SCHUMANN. Five Hunting Songs. op. 137. TTBB.
4 hns. Ger. Text: Heinrich Laube. Eng. Jean
Lunn. (1) In Praise of Hunting, (2) Be Intent, (3)
Morning, (4) Daybreak, (5) Drinking Song. CFP
#6614. (10:00)

211 SCHUMANN. Intermezzo, und schläfst du, op. 74, no.
2. TB. pf. Ger. Text: Geibel. (from the Spanischen Liebes-Liedern). CFP #2392. (1:00)

212 SCHUMANN. Ritornelle, op. 65 (Canons). unac. Ger.
Texts: Rückert. (1) Die Rose stand im Tau,
TTBBB, (3:30); (2) Lasst Lautenspiel und Becherk-
lang, BB; (3) Blüt oder Schnee, TTT-TTBB; (4)
Gebt mir zu Trinken, BBB; (5) Zürne nicht des
Herbstes Wind, TTBB; (6) Im Sommertagen rüste
den Schlitten, TTBB; (7) In Merres Mitten ist ein
Off'ner Laden, TTBB. CFP.

213 SCHUMANN. The Rose Stood in the Dew (Die Rose
stand im Tau), op. 65, no. 1, ed. Carl Pfatteicher.
TTBBB. unac. Eng. Dirk H. van der Stucken.
Ger. Fredrick Rückert. CF#CM 2109. (3:30)

214 SCHUMANN. Sechs Lieder für vierstimmigen Männer-
chor, op. 33. TTBB. unac. Ger. (1) Der Trau-
mende See. Text: J. Mosen. (2) Die Minnesänger.
Text: H. Heine. (3) Die Lotusblume. Text: H.
Heine. (4) Der Zecher als Doktrinar. Text: J.
Mosen. (5) Rastlose Liebe. Text: Goethe. (6)
Frühlingsglocken. Text: Reinick. CFP #EP
2527A

215 STANFORD, CHARLES (1852-1924). Songs of the Sea.
TTBB (ad lib.). B. solo. pf. Eng. Text: Henry
Newbolt. BH. (17:00) 5 Mvts: (1) Drake's Drum,
(2) Outward Bound, (3) Devon, O Devon, in Wind
and Rain, (4) Homeward Bound, (5) The Old Superb.

216 STRAUSS, RICHARD (1864-1949). Austria, op. 78.
TB. orch. reduced for pf. Ger. Text: Anton
Wildgans. BB

217 STRAUSS. Schwäbische Erbschaft. TTBB. Ger. Text:

Feodor Löwe. LC #135. (2:00)

218 SULLIVAN, SIR ARTHUR (1842-1900). Entrance and March of the Peers; Iolanthe. TTBB. pf. 4 hands. Eng. Text: Gilbert. ECS #91. (5:15)

219 SULLIVAN. With Cat Like Tread (Come Friends Who Plough the Sea); Pirates of Penzance. TTBB. pf. Eng. Text: Gilbert. GS. (2:30)

220 TCHAIKOVSKY, PETER (1840-1893). Now If Pretty Girls Had Wings (Tomsky's Song, 2nd Gambler's chorus); The Queen of Spades. TTBB. Bar. solo. pf. Text: Eng. trans. Arthur Jacobs. OX #M11

221 VERDI, GIUSSEPPE (1813-1901). Allegri, beviam (The Bandits Chorus); Ernani. TTBB. pf. It. Text: Francesco Piave. RIC

222 VERDI. Hush, Come Quickly (Zitti, zitti, moviamo a vendetta); Rigoletto, arr. B. Fitzgerald. TTBB. pf. It. Text: Francesco Piave. Eng. Bernard Fitzgerald. FC #NY145. Also FC #NY470, It. ed. Northcote.

223 VERDI. La Vergine degl'angeli, Finale, Act II (Coro di frati); La Forza del destino. TTBB. pf. S. T. & B. solos. It. Text: Francesco Piave. RIC

224 VERDI. Miserere; Il Trovatore. TTBB. pf. S. & T. solos. It. (includes recitative and aria: D'amor sull'ali rosee). Text: S. Cammarano. Eng. Natalia Macfarren. GS #6977. (Miserere only: 3:35)

225 VERDI. All'erta! All'erta!; Il Trovatore (Act I, sc. 1, complete). TTBB. B. solo. pf. It. Text: S. Cammarano. Eng. Text: Natalia MacFarren. GS. (9:30)

226 VERDI. Soldiers' Chorus; Il Trovatore, (Act III). TTBB. pf. It. Eng. Text: S. Cammarano. NOV #41 (4:00)

227 VERDI. Macbeth: Trema Banco, Act II (Coro di si- cari: Chi vi'impose unirvi a noi?). TTBB. It. Text: Piave. RIC. (3:00)

228 WAGNER, RICHARD (1813-1883). Battle Hymn; Rienzi.
     TTBB.   pf. Eng. Text: Wagner.   GS #1180

229 WAGNER. Die Meistersinger: Act III, sc. 5.   March
     of the Shoemakers (Sankt Krispin lobet ihn).   TTBB;
     March of the Tailors (Als Nürenberg).   TTBB;
     March of the Bakers (Hungersnoth).   TTBB.   Ger.
     Text: Wagner.   Eng. Frederick Jameson.   GS

230 WAGNER. Gralsfeier (Feast of the Holy Grail): Par-
     sifal, Act I (Zum letzten Liebesmahle), arr. Richard
     Schmidt.   TTBB.   pf. 4 hands.   Ger. Text: Wag-
     ner.   Eng. trans. Dr. Th. Baker.   BMC

231 WAGNER. Lohengrin: Act III, sc. 2, In Früh'n ver-
     sammelt.   TTBB-TTBB.   Ger. Eng. (entire scene
     very effective, would include short solos for B. and
     solo TTB).   Text: Wagner.   GS

232 WAGNER. Pilgrims' Chorus: Tannhauser.   TTBB.
     pf. Eng. Ger. Text: Wagner.   GS #1164.   (1:30)

233 WAGNER. Procession of Knights; Parsifal, arr. Mc-
     Conathy.   TTBB.   pf. 4 hands.   Ger. Text: Wag-
     ner.   Eng. McConathy.   NOV

234 WAGNER. Steersman, Leave the Watch; The Flying
     Dutchman.   TTBB.   pf. Ger. Text: Wagner. Eng.
     Th. Baker.   GS #1164

235 WEBER, CARL MARIA VON (1786-1826).   Der Freis-
     chütz: Was gleicht auf Erden.   (Hunter's chorus).
     TTBB.   pf. Ger. Text: Fredrich Kind.   MCA.

236 WEBER.   Song of Slumber (Schlummerlied), ed. Plott.
     TTBB.   unac.   Eng. Ger. Text: Anon.   BR #DC2

              IMPRESSIONISTS and POST-IMPRESSIONISTS

237 CAPLET, ANDRE (1878-1925).   Messe à Trois Voix.
     unac.   Lat.   DUR.   (20:00)

238 DEBUSSY, CLAUDE (1862-1918).   Invocation.   TTBB.

pf. T. solo. Fr. Text: Alphonse de Lamartine.
CFP #C3. (5:30)

239 DURUFLE, MAURICE (1902-). Messe Cum Jubilo.
unis. B. solo. org. (and orch.). Lat. Text:
Mass. DUR.

240 IBERT, JACQUES (1890-1962). Deux Chants de Carnaval.
3 ev. unac. Fr. Text: Machiavelli. HEU.

241 POULENC, FRANCIS (1899-1963). Chanson à boire.
TTBB. unac. Fr. Text: Jean Victor Hugo. SAL.
(3:30)

242 POULENC. Clic, Clac, Dansez Sabots. TTB. unac.
Fr. Text: Fr. Folk. SAL. (1:45)

243 POULENC. LaBelle si nous étions. TTB. unac. Fr.
Folk. SAL. (1:15)

244 POULENC. Laudes de Saint Antoine de Padoue. 1.
O Jesu. (1:45). 2. O Proles. (0:45). 3. Laus
regi. (2:00). 4. Si quaeris. (2:00). TBB. unac.
Fr. Text: St. Anthony. SAL

245 POULENC. Quatre Prières de Saint François D'Assise.
(1) Salut, Dame Sainte. TBB. (2:00). (2) Tout
Puissant, très Saint. TBBB. (1:15). (3) Seigneur,
je vous en prie. TBB. (1:15). (4) O mes très
Chers Frères. TBBB. T. solo. (1:15). all unac.
Fr. Text: St. Francis of Assisi. SAL

246 POULENC. Sept répons des Tenebres. Although written for male voices, the work requires boys' voices.
It is difficult to extract all-male sections; nevertheless, it is an interesting work.

247 ROUSSEL, ALBERT (1869-1937). LeBardit des Francs.
TTBB. 2 tr. C, 2 hns. F, 3 tromb., tuba, timp.
perc. Fr. Text: 6th C. Book of Martyrs by
Chateaubriand. DUR. (6:00)

CONTEMPORARY

248 ANDRIESSEN, HENDRIK (1892-). Missa Fiat Volun-
     tas Tua.   TB.   org.   Lat.   GI #1002

249 ANDRIESSEN.   Missa Sanctus Ludovicus.   3 ev.   unac.
     org.   Lat.   WL

250 ANDRIESSEN.   Missa Sponsa Christi.   3 ev.   unac.
     Lat.   VRH

251 ARGENTO, Dominick (1927-).   The Revelation of
     Saint John the Divine, Rhapsody for Tenor, male
     chorus, brass and percussion.   TTBB.   solos; ex-
     tended T. solo.   pf. reduction (Brass: 3 hns. F,
     2 tr. C, 2 tromb. 2 perc. pf. harp).   Eng. Text:
     John.   Part 1: Prologue and Adoration; Part 2:
     The Seven Seals and Seven Trumpets; Part 3:
     Jubilation and Epilogue.   BH.   (36:00)

252 BACON, ERNST (1898-).   Seven Canons.   2-4 ev.
     pf. Eng.   (1) God. Text: Angelus Silesius.   trans.
     Paul Carus.   (2) Sinai.   Text: Talmud.   (3)
     Schools and Rules.   Text: William Blake.   (4)
     The Pelican.   Text: unknown.   (5) The Little Chil-
     dren.   Text: Talmud.   (6) Chop-Cherry.   Text:
     Robert Herrick.   (7) Money.   Text: unknown.
     MMC #352-00114.

253 BANTOCK, GRANVILLE (1868-1946).   She Walks in
     Beauty.   TTBB.   unac. Eng. Text: Byron.   NOV
     #656

254 BANTOCK.   Silent Strings.   TTBB.   pf. Eng. Text:
     Helen Taylor.   BH #1455.   (2:15)

255 BARTOK, BELA (1881-1945).   Five Slovak Folk Songs.
     TTBB.   unac. Text: Slovak-Hungarian Folk.   Eng.
     trans. Nancy Bush.   Ger. trans. Mirko Jelusich.
     Hung. trans. Wanda Gleiman.   BH #17682.   (6:30)

256 BARTOK.   Four Old Hungarian Folksongs.   TTBB.
     unac. Eng. trans. Matyas Seiber and Leo Black.
     BH #5575.   (6:00)

257 BENJAMIN, ARTHUR (1893-1960).   To a Wine Jug.

TTBB. pf. Eng. Text: Anon. Greek, trans. A. C.
Benson. BH #5249

258 BLISS, ARTHUR (1891-   ). Two Songs from the film,
The Beggar's Opera, 1953, arr. Bliss. TTBB.
pf. Eng. Text: unknown. (1) Let Us Take the
Road, (2) Fill Ev'ry Glass. NOV #703.

259 BRITTEN, BENJAMIN (1913-   ). Rustics and Fisher-
man; Gloriana. unac. Eng. Text: W. Plomer.
BH #5017

260 BRITTEN. The Ballad of Little Musgrave and Lady
Barnard. TBB. pf. Eng. Text: Anon. Oxford
Book of Ballads. BH #1992. (12:00)

261 BUSONI, FERRUCCIO (1866-1924). Concerto in C Major for Piano and Orchestra with final chorus for
Male Chorus, op. 39. Text: Hymn to Pillah, from
the play Alladin, Oehlenschlager. pub. Breitkopf.

262 CASALS, PABLO (1876-   ). Nigra sum (I Am Black).
TTB. pf. org. Lat. Text: Eng. vers. Kenneth
Sterne. ALB #240-8. (5:00)

263 CHAMPAGNE, CLAUDE (1891-1965). Ave Maria.
TBB. unac. Lat. Text: Luke 1:28. BMI-C #182.
(2:00)

264 CHAMPAGNE. Missa Brevis à Trois Voix. unac.
Lat. BMI-C

265 COUTURE, JEAN PAPINEAU (1916-   ). Laudate eum;
Psalm 150. TTBB. 3 tr. 3 tromb. org. Lat.
BMI-C. (3:00)

266 COUTURE. Te mater alma. TBB. unac. Lat. Text:
Anon. Lauds Hymn. SMC (1:30)

267 CRUFT, ADRIAN (1921-   ). May God Abide, op. 20.
TTBB. unac. Eng. Text: John 4:16. SB #5667.
(1:30)

268 CRUFT. Thy God Was Making Haste. TTBB. unac.
Eng. Text: Richard Crashaw. SB #5667

269 DELIUS, FREDERICK (1862-1934). Wanderer's Song.

TTBB. (Some div. in all parts). pf. Eng. Ger.
Text: Ger. R. S. Hoffman. Eng. Arthur Symons.
BH #1634

270 ELGAR, SIR EDWARD (1857-1934). Five Part Songs
from the Greek Anthology, op. 45. (1) Yea, Cast
Me From Heights of the Mountain. Text: Anon.
Greek. Eng. trans. Alma Strettel. (2) Whether I
Find Thee. Text: Anon. Greek. Eng. trans.
Andrew Lang. (3) After Many a Dusty Mile. Text:
Anon. Greek. Eng. trans. Edmund Gosse. (4) It's
Oh! To Be a Wild Wind. Text: Anon. Greek.
Eng. trans. W. M. Hardinge. (5) Feasting I Watch.
Marcus Argentarius. Eng. trans. Richard Garnett.
All TTBB. unac. Ger. trans. Julius Buths. NOV.

271 ELGAR. Zut! Zut! Zut! (Remember). TTBB. unac.
Eng. Text: Richard Mardon. NOV #591

272 ELGAR. The Reveille. TTBB. unac. Eng. Text:
Bret Harte. NOV #449

273 FINZI, GERALD (1901-1956). Thou Dids't Delight My
Eyes. TBB. Text: Robert Bridges. BH #5456

274 GERMAN, EDWARD (1862-1936). O Peaceful Night.
TTBB. unac. Eng. Text: W. Herbert Scott. NOV
#497

275 GINASTERA, ALBERTO (1916-). Arriero, Canta
(Sing Muleteer). TTBB. unac. Eng. Sp. Text:
Felix Errico. Eng. Lorraine Finley. BMC #2968

276 GRETCHANINOFF, ALEXANDER (1864-1956). The
Cherubic Hymn, arr. by the composer. TTBB.
unac. Eng. Text: Russian Liturgy of St. John
Chrysostum. JF #8667. (3:30)

277 GRETCHANINOFF. Glory to God. TTBB. unac.
Eng. Text: Gloria; Mass Text. EBM #53. (3:15)

278 HINDEMITH, PAUL (1895-1963). The Demon of the
Gibbet (Galgenritt). TBB. unac. Eng. Ger. Text:
Fitz-James O'Brien. SCH #37535

279 HINDEMITH. Der Tod. unac. Ger. Text: Friedrich
Hölderlin. SCH #33527

280 HINDEMITH. Du Musst dir Alles geben. unac. Ger.
Text: Gottfried Benn. SCH #32784

281 HINDEMITH. Eine lichte Mitternacht. TTBB. unac.
Text: Walt Whitman. Ger. trans. Johannes Schlaf.
SCH #32548

282 HINDEMITH. Erster Schnee. TTBB. unac. Ger.
Text: Gottfried Keller. SCH #37483

283 HINDEMITH. Fürst Kraft. TTBB. unac. Ger. Text:
Gottfried Benn. SCH #32783

284 HINDEMITH. Uber das Früjahr. TTBB. unac. Ger.
Text: Bertolt Brecht. SCH #32545

285 HINDEMITH. Variationen über ein altes Tanzlied (Das
jung auch das alte). TTBB. unac. Ger. Text:
Old German. SCH #37584

286 HINDEMITH. Vision des Mannes. TTBB. unac. Ger.
Text: Gottfried Benn. SCH 32785

287 HOLST, GUSTAV (1864-1934). Before Sleep. TB
(canon). org. or pf. Eng. Text: Helen Waddell,
from the Latin of Prudentius. WR

288 HOLST. Choral Hymns from the Rig Veda (Fourth
Group), op. 26. TTBB. orch. reduction for pf.
Eng. (1) Hymn to Agni (the sacrificial fire).
(2) Hymn to Soma (Soma is the juice of a herb
used in sacrifice). (3) Hymn to Manas (an invocation to the Manas or spirit of a dying man). (4)
Hymn to Indra (Indra is the God of heaven, storm,
and battle). GR #291, 292, 293, 294

289 HOLST. Good Friday. TTBB. pf. or org. Eng.
Text: Helen Waddell from the Lat. of Peter Abelard. BH #5294

290 HOLST. Dirge for Two Veterans. TTBB. pf. or 2
tr. B-flat, 2 tromb. (or tromb. or tuba), side
drum, bass drum. Text: Walt Whitman. GS
#8323. (instrumental parts on rental).

291 HOLST. How Mighty Are the Sabbaths. TTBB. org.
(pf.) Eng. Text: Helen Waddell, from the Latin of
Peter Abelard. BH #3031

292 HOLST. Intercession. TTBB.   pf. (org.) Eng. Text:
     Helen Waddell. BH #5360

293 HOLST. I Vow Thee My Country. (Melody taken from
     Jupitor, no. 4 of The Planets). unis. pf. Eng.
     Text: Sir C. S. Rice. GS #11334

294 HOLST. Song of the Lumberman. 2 pts. pf. Eng.
     Text: John G. Whittier. OX

295 HOLST. Song of the Shipbuilders. 2 ev. Eng. Text:
     Whittier. OX

296 HONEGGER, ARTHUR (1892-1955). King David: Song
     of the Prophets. TB. pf. Fr. Text: René Morax.
     Eng. Edward Agate. FF. (1:15)

297 KAHN, ERICH ITOR (1905-1956). Rhapsodie Hassidique.
     TTBB. unac. (if the intonation problems are ex-
     treme the composer has provided a wind instru-
     mentation: E. Hn. cl. in A, Bcl. bn. 2 hns. F,
     tromb. org.). Heb. Text: Traditional Hassidic.
     ACA

298 KODALY, ZOLTAN (1882-1967). The Bachelor. TBB.
     unac. Text: Folk Song from Szekelg. Eng. vers.
     Nancy Bush. BH #1893

299 KODALY. Drinking Song. TTBB. unac. Eng. Text:
     orig. Hung. Ferenc Kilcsey. Eng. trans. Matyas
     Seiber, Leo Black. TP #7445A. (6:00)

300 KODALY. Evening Song. TBB. unac. Text: Eng.
     trans. Geoffrey Russell-Smith. BH #5798

301 KODALY. The Peacocks. TBB. unac. Eng. trans.
     Nancy Bush. BH #1894. (3:00)

302 KODALY. The Ruins. TBB. unac. Text: Eng. vers.
     Elizabeth M. Lockwood. UN #312-405595. (3:00)

303 KODALY. Soldier's Song. TBB. tr. snare drum.
     Text: Eng. vers. Nancy Bush. BH #1892. (3:30)

304 KODALY. Songs from Karad. TBB. unac. Eng.
     trans. Nancy Bush. BH #1894. (5:00)

305 KODALY. Tavern Song. TTBB. unac. Eng. Text:
     Anon 17th Cent. Eng. trans. Matyas Seiber, Leo
     Black. TP #7445B. (2:15)

306 KRENEK, ERNST (1900-). Missa Duodecim Tonorum.
     TTB. org. Lat. (Rare instance of a 12-Tone
     Mass). GI #1001

307 LANGLAIS, JEAN (1907-). Mass God Have Mercy,
     unis. org. Eng. MCR #2577

308 LANGLAIS. Missa Dona Nobis Pacem. unis. org.
     Eng. NOV #2836

309 LANGLAIS. Missa Salve Regina. TTB, people's unis.
     chorus. 3 tr. 5 tromb. 2 org. Lat. ECP. (18:00)

310 LANGLAIS. Psalm 150. TTB. org. Eng. MCR
     #2203. (3:00)

311 LEVY, ERNST (1895-). Hear, Ye Children. TBB-
     TBB. unac. Eng. Text: Proverbs 4: 1, 7, 8.
     ALB #BCS1

312 MALIPIERO, G. FRANCESCO (1882-). Universa Uni-
     versis. TB. reduction for pf. Orch: 2 fl. 2 ob.
     2 bn. 4 hns. 2 vns. 2 va. 2 vc. Text: Medieval
     Goliard Lyrics. SZ. (15:00)

313 MARTINU, BOHUSLAV (1890-1959). Field Mass. (Al-
     so known as Military Mass). TTBB. B. solo.
     Instrumentation: 2 fl. (picc.); 2 cl. in B-flat, 3
     tr. in C, timp. gr. cassa; piatti; tamburo piccolo
     (con corda and senza timbro); tambura military
     cratolo; triangle; Mass bells; bells (ad lib.); har-
     monium; pf. Slovak. Text: Ps. 44, 42, and
     original words by Jiri Mucha. On rental. Miltan-
     trich, Prague. BH. (20:00)

314 MAWBY, COLIN (1938-). O Come, Let Us Sing Unto
     the Lord. 2 ev. org. Eng. GI #1098. (1) Ps.
     95, vs. 1-5; (2) Ps. 137, vs. 1-4; (3) Ps. 101,
     vs. 1-4; (4) Ps. 148, vs. 1-5.

315 MILHAUD, DARIUS (1892-). Agamemnon. TTBB
     (some div.). S. Solo pf. 4 hands. Fr. Text:
     Paul Claudel. Publishers: Heugel, Paris, c/o TP

316 MILHAUD. Psalm 121. TTBB. unac. Fr. Eng. Ger.
     Text: Paul Claudel. UN #9632

317 NIELAND, JAN (1903-). Prayer of St. Francis.
     TB. org. Text: St. Francis. WL #ESA 512-2

318 ORFF, CARL (1895-). Carmina Burana: In Taberna
     (Part II) (The entire part II is effective as a unit).
     TTBB. pf. T & B solos. Lat. Text: 13th Cent.
     Student Songs. (1) Estuans interius. solo Bar.
     no chorus, (2:00). (2) Olim lacus colueram. solo
     T. TBB, (3:30). (3) Ego sum abbas. solo. Bar.
     TTBB, (2:30). (4) In Taberna quando sumas.
     TBB, (3:30) SCH

319 ORFF. Carmina Burana: Cours d'Amours (Part III),
     Si puer cum puellula. TTTBBB. pf. Lat. Text:
     13 Cent. Student Song. SCH. (1:00)

320 ORFF. Sunt lacrimae rerum; Concento di voci.
     BBBBB (or TTTBBB). TBB solos. unac. Lat.
     (1) Omnium deliciarum. Text: Orlando di Lasso.
     (2) Omnia tempus habent. Text: Ecclesiastes 3:
     1-8. (3) Eripe nos. Text: trans. Rudolf Bach.
     SCH #39 534. (13:00)

321 PEETERS, FLOR (1903-). The Confraternity Mass.
     unis. org. Eng. MCR #2568

322 PEETERS. Entrata festiva. unis. 2 tr. 2 tromb.
     org. Lat. Text: attr. Charlemagne. CFP #6159.
     (7:00)

323 PEETERS. Jubilate Deo. TTB. org. Lat. Eng.
     Text: Ps. 99. MCR #1893

324 PEETERS. Magnificat. TTB. org. Lat. Text: Luke
     1: 46-56. MCR #2527

325 PEETERS. Missa in Honorem Reginae Pacis. TB.
     org. Lat. MCR #1692

326 PEETERS. Missa in Honorem Sancti Lutgardis. TB.
     org. Lat. MCR #1758

327 PEETERS. Te Deum. TT(B)B. org. Lat. Eng.
     Text: Nicetas, Bishop, ca. 400. MCR #1484.
     (5:00)

328 PEROSI, LORENZO (1872-1956). Missa Te Deum Laudamus. TB. org. Lat. RIC

329 PITFIELD, THOMAS (1903-). A Sketchbook for Men. TBB. Bar. solo. pf. opt. perc. (or str. pf. perc.). Eng. Text: Pitfield. HEL #268. (25:00)

330 PITFIELD. Evening Service for Men's Voices: Magnificat and Nunc dimittis. TTBB. org. Eng. Text: Luke I: 46-56 and Song of Simeon, Luke 2: 29-32. HEL #882

331 PITFIELD. Miniatures: (1) The Village Bell, (2) The Needle, (3) The Windmill. 2 ev. pf. opt. perc. (glockenspiel, chime bars or bells.) Eng. Text: Pitfield HEL #266A. (1:00 ea.)

332 PITFIELD. Two Metrical Psalms: Ps. 23 (paraphrased by Addison); Ps. 127, unis. pf. or org. Eng. HEL #H556B. (4:00, 2:30)

333 SCHONBERG, ARNOLD (1865-1951). Six Pieces for Male Chorus, op. 35. TTBB: Restraint (Hemmung); The Law (Das Gesetz); Means of Expression (Ausdruckweise); Happiness (Gluck); Obligation (Landsknechte); Yeomen (Verbundenheit). unac. Text: Ger. Schönberg. Eng. trans. D. Millar Craig and Adolph Weiss. BB

334 SCHONBERG. A Survivor from Warsaw, op. 46. men's unis. narrator. orch. (Picc. 2-2-2-2-; 4-3-3-1; xylophone; bells; chimes; military drums; B dr.; timp.; cymbals; triangle; tamb.; tam-tam; castanets; hp. strings). Chorus in Heb. Narrator text by Schönberg in Eng.: Fr. text, René Leibowitz; Gr. text, Margaret Peter. Bomart. (6:00)

335 SERLY, TIBOR (1901-). Hymn of Nativity. TTBB. unac. Eng. Text: Richard Crashaw. SOU

336 SERLY. The Good Time Coming. TTBBB. unac. Eng. Text: Charles Mackay. SOU # ME1008

337 SIBELIUS, JEAN (1865-1957). Forest Invocation (Metsamiehen Laulu), op. 15 no. 5, ed. Richard D. Row. TTBB. unac. Eng. Text: R. Row. ROW #316. (1:30)

338 SIBELIUS. Hymne, op. 21, no. 2. (same as Natus
     in Curas). TTBB. unac. Lat. Text: Gustafsson.
     BHW #2007. (4:30)

339 SIBELIUS. Song of the Athenians, op. 31A. boys and
     men. 6 hns. perc.

340 SIBELIUS. Vale of Tuoni (Sydameni Laulu), ed. Richard
     Row. TTBB. pf. Finnish text: A. Kivi. Eng.
     R. Row. ROW #310. (2:30)

341 SIBELIUS. Natus in curas (Mortal Man Born to Sor-
     row and Tribulation), op. 21 no. 2, ed. Richard
     Row. TTBB. unac. Lat. Text: Eng. trans. R.
     D. Row. CF #348. (4:30)

342 SOWANDE, FELA (1905-). The Gramercy of Sleep.
     TTBB. unac. Eng. Text: C. S. Andrews. RIC
     #NY2115

343 SOWANDE. Words. TTBB. unac. Eng. Text: C. S.
     Andrews. RIC #NY21114

344 STRAVINSKY, IGOR (1882-1971). Babel. Cantata
     From the Book of Moses I, Capital II, vs. 1-9.
     Male chorus. narrator (male). Lat. Orch: 3 fl.
     (picc.), 2 ob. 2 cl. B-flat, Bcl. 2 bn. Bbn. 4 hns.
     F, 3 tr. C, 3 tromb. timp. harp, str. Also avail-
     able in pf. score (2 pianos). BEL. (7:00)

345 STRAVINSKY. Four Russian Folksongs. TTBB. un-
     ac. (also with 4 hns.). Eng. Fr. Text: Russian
     Folk. (1) On Saint's Day in Chigisakh, (2) Ovsen,
     (3) The Pike, (4) Master Portly. CHES #27. (1:00,
     0:35; 1:00; 1:15).

346 STRAVINSKY. Introitus, T. S. Eliot in Memoriam.
     TB. harp, pf. 2 tam-tams (H and L), timp. (2
     players) va. stb. Text: from the Requiem Mass.
     BH. (4:00)

347 STRAVINSKY. Le Roi des Etoiles. TTBB. orch.
     reduced for pf. Russian. Text: Constantin Bal-
     mont. Fr. trans. Michel Calvocoressi. CFP #F-
     94. (6:30)

348 STRAVINSKY. Oedipus Rex, opera-oratorio in two

acts after Sophocles. TTBB. Solos: T., Mezzo,
Bar., B. and T., speaker. (Orch: 3 fl. 2 ob.
Eng. hn. 3 cl. A, 2 bns. Bbn. 4 hns. F, 4 tr. C,
3 tromb., tuba, timp. perc. harp, pf. str.). Re-
duction for pf. by the composer. Text: adap. into
Fr. by Jean Cocteau. trans. Lat. J. Danieleu.
Eng. trans. of the speaker's text by E. E. Cum-
mings. BH. (50:00)

349 STRUBE, GUSTAV. Hymns to Eros, op. 19. TTBB.
T. solo. pf. Text: Ger. C. A. Köhler. Eng.
vers. George L. Osgood. BMC

350 TCHEREPNIN, A. (1899-). Mass for Three Equal
Voices. TTB. unac. Eng. CFP #66162

351 TOCH, ERNST (1887-1964). Geographical Fugue for
Speaking Chorus. SATB (possible TTBB). Eng.
Text: Toch (?). MM #60-168

352 VAUGHAN WILLIAMS, RALPH (1872-1958). Drinking
Song (Back and Side Go Bare); Sir John in Love.
TTBB. pf. Eng. Text: John Still. OX

353 VAUGHAN WILLIAMS. Five Tudor Portraits: Epitaph
on John Jayberd of Diss. TB (some div.). pf.
Eng. Text: John Skelton. OX. (3:30)

354 VAUGHAN WILLIAMS. Let Us Now Praise Famous
Men. unis. pf. (org.). Text: Ecclesiastes. CUR

355 VAUGHAN WILLIAMS. The Vagabond. TTBB. unac.
Eng. Text: Robert Louis Stevenson. BH #5454

356 VILLA-LOBOS, HEITOR. Choros #3 (Pica-Pao).
TTBB. cl. A. Sax. bn. 3 hns. 3 tromb. Text:
Port. -Indian Dialect. AMP. (6:00)

357 VILLA-LOBOS. Na Bahia Tem. TTBB. unac. Port.
Text: unknown. EME. (2:00)

358 VILLA-LOBOS. Mass in Honor of Saint Sebastian
(Missa São Sebastião). TTB. unac. Lat. AMP.
(24:00)

359 WILLAN, HEALEY (1880-1970). Missa Brevis. TTBB.
unac. Eng. CON #63118

360 WILLAN. Welcome Yule. TTBB. S. solo. unac.
     Eng. Text: Anon. English 15th Cent. BMI-C
     #3208

361 WYTON, ALEC (1921-). Benedictus es Domine and
     Jubilate Deo. TTB. unac. Eng. Text: Dan. 3:
     52-56. CON #98-1729; 98-1595

362 WYTON. Mass to Honor St. John the Divine. TTBB.
     cong. org. Eng. WL # EMO-865-8

CONTEMPORARY AMERICANS

363 ADLER, SAMUEL (1928-). Begin, My Muse. TTBB.
     6 perc. players: xylophone; marimba: 5 tom-toms;
     5 wood blocks; suspended cymbals; drums; vibra-
     phone; snare drum; tambourine; glockenspiel. Eng.
     (1) Love. Text: Anacreon and Anacreonties. trans.
     Robert Herrick. (2) Brown Penny. Text: W. B.
     Yeats. (3) Lyric. Text: Gil Orlovitz. (4) The
     Eye. Text: Robert Creeley. (5) The Poet Speaks.
     Text: Georgia Douglas Johnson. OX, on rental.

364 ADLER. Two Songs of Hope. 1. Psalm 121 (I Will
     Lift Mine Eyes up to the Mountain). TTBB. org.
     Eng. 2. God Is My Salvation. TTBB. org. Eng.
     Text: Isaiah, 12: 2, 1, 3-6. MMC #430

365 AVSHALOMOV, JACOB (1919-). Proverbs of Hell.
     TTBBBB. Narrator. unac. Eng. Text: William
     Blake. ACA. Also MCA. (6:00)

366 BALLANTINE, EDWARD (1886-). The House Among
     the Trees: Stockbridge. TTBB. pf. Eng. Text:
     J. L. McLane, Jr. ECS #65

367 BARBER, SAMUEL (1910-). A Nun Takes the Veil.
     TTBB. unac. Eng. Text: Gerard Manley Hopkins.
     GS #10859. (1:30)

368 BARBER. A Stopwatch and an Ordnance Map. TTBB.
     (some div.). 3 timp. T. and B. solos. Eng. Text:
     Stephen Spender. GS #8799. (5:30). (parts for

optional accompaniment: 4 hns. 3 tromb. tuba
available on rental.)

369 BARLOW, WAYNE (1912-). Diversify the Abyss.
TTBB. pf. Eng. Text: Hyam Plutzik. TP #312-
40570

370 BARROW, ROBERT (1911-). Hush My Dear, Lie
Still and Slumber. TTBB. unac. Eng. Text:
Isaac Watts. ECS #2173

371 BARROW. Three Psalms of Penitence: Out of the
Deep, Ps. 130; Bow Down Thine Ear, Ps. 86;
Show Me Thy Ways, O Lord, Ps. 25. TTBB.
org. Eng. Texts: Psalms. Unpublished. Available
from CAP

372 BEESON, JACK (1921-). Everyman's Handyman. 9
rounds and canons for men's voices: (1) To Cure
a Kicking Cow, (2) To Prevent Flies from Injuring
Picture Frames, (3) Against Taking Poison Acci-
dentally, (4) Against Falling Asleep in Church, (5)
To Remove Moles and Warts, (6) Potatoes as Paste
and Pen-Wipers, (7) To Rid Yourself of Rats With
Poison, (8) An Excellent Cement, (9) To Revive a
Chilled Pig. unac. Eng. Text: Elizabeth W.
Smith. BH #5817

373 BEESON. In Praise of Bloomers. TTBB. unac.
Eng. Text: Anon. BH #5754

374 BENDER, JAN (1909-). Begone, Satan (from the
Gospel for Invocavit, First Sunday in Lent). 2
ev. org. Eng. Text: Matt. 15: 4-10. CON #98-
1848

375 BENDER. Come, O Blessed of My Father (from
the Gospel, Trinity 26). 2 ev. org. Eng. Text:
Matt. 15: 25-34. CON #98-1834

376 BENDER. It Is Not Fair (from the Gospel, Second
Sunday in Lent). 2 ev. org. Eng. Text: Matt.
15: 26-28. CON #98-1833

377 BENDER. Lord, Lord, Open to Us (from the Gospel,
Trinity 27). unis. org. Eng. Text: Matt. 25: 11-
13. CON #98-1833

378 BENDER.   Sir, Come Down Before My Child Dies
     (from the Gospel, Trinity 21). 2 ev. org. Eng.
     Text: John 4: 49-50. CON #98-1835

379 BERGER, JEAN (1912-).   Hope for Tomorrow.
     TTBB. pf. Eng. Text: Martin Luther King, Jr.
     GS #10727

380 BERGER.   I've Known Rivers. TTBB. unac. Eng.
     Text: Langston Hughes. ROW #518. (5:30)

381 BERGER.   Old Moby Dick. TTBB. pf. Eng. Text:
     W. Storrs Lee. ROW #532. (3:00)

382 BERGER.   She'd Be Good If She Could But She Can't.
     TTBB. pf. Eng. Text: W. Storrs Lee. ROW
     #533. (2:15)

383 BERGER.   Three Fancies: The Bounty of Our Age;
     On a Spark of Fire Fixing on a Gentlewoman's
     Breast; If All The World Were Paper. TTBB. pf.
     Eng. Text: 1, Farley, 1621; 2, Philipott, 1641;
     3, Anon. 1641. ROW #517

384 BERGSMA, WILLIAM (1921-).   Let True Love Among
     Us Be. TB. pf. Eng. Text: 13th Cent. Anon.
     modern text, Nancy Bush. CF#CM 6534. (2:00)

385 BERNSTEIN, LEONARD (1918-).   Pirate Song: Peter
     Pan. TTBB. Bar. solo. pf. Eng. Text: Bern-
     stein. GS #9915

386 BEVERIDGE, THOMAS (1938-).   Drop, Drop, Slow
     Tears. TTBB. pf. Eng. Text: Phineas Fletcher.
     ECS #2174

387 BINKERD, GORDON (1916-).   Alleluia for St. Fran-
     cis. TB. org. Eng. Text: Roman-Sephardic
     Missal. BH #5686. (4:00)

388 BINKERD.   And Viva Sweet Love. TBB. pf. 4 hands.
     Eng. Text: E. E. Cummings. BH #5750. (5:00)

389 BINKERD.   Dum medium silentium. TTBB. unac.
     Lat. Text: Wisdom: 18:14, 15. (Introit, Sunday
     within the Octave of Christmas). BH #5630.
     (4:00)

390 BINKERD. From Your Throne, O Lord. unison.
org. Eng. Text: Ps: 79, 2 (3rd Sunday of Advent).
BH #5826

391 BINKERD. Let My Prayer Come Like Incense. TB.
org. Eng. Text: Ps. 140: 2 (Gradual, 19th Sunday
after Pentecost). BH #5828

392 BINKERD. Liebeslied (The Song of Love). TTBB.
unac. Ger. Eng. Text: Rainer Maria Rilke. BH
#5631. (4:00)

393 BINKERD. Songs from the Silver Tassie. TBB. pf.
Eng. Text: Sean O'Casey. BH #5830

394 BINKERD. There Is a Garden In Her Face. TBB.
unac. Eng. Text: Thomas Campion, The Fourth
Book of Ayres (1610-12). BH #5836

395 BLITZSTEIN, MARC (1905-1964). Invitation to Bitter-
ness. TTBB. pf. Eng. Text: Blitzstein. ARROW.
(3:00)

396 CARTER, ELLIOTT (1908-). The Defense of Co-
rinth. TTBB. speaker. pf. four hands. Eng.
Text: Rabelais. MMC #54. (17:00)

397 CARTER. Emblems. TTBB. pf. Eng. Text: Allen
Tate. MMC #MP 120. (16:00)

398 CLOKEY, JOSEPH (1890-1960). Holiday Cruise, choral
cycle for TTBB. pf. Eng. Text: Willis Knapp
Jones. (1) An Invitation, CF #9053; (2) The De-
parture, CF #9054; (3) Dawn at Sea, CF #9055;
(4) The Cloud Ship, CF #9056.

399 CLOKEY. Souvenir. TTBB. unac. Eng. Text: Clay-
ton C. Quest. CF #6119

400 CONVERSE, FREDERICK (1871-1940). Laudate Dominum. TBB. 2 tr. F, 3 T. tromb. and B. tromb.
ad lib. org. (possible to play only with org.). Lat.
Text: Ps. 148. BMC #228

401 COPLAND, AARON (1900-). Old American Songs,
Set I (adapted by Copland, Wilding-White, Fine)
(1) The Boatmen's Dance. TTBB. pf. Eng. Text:

Minstrel-Folk Song, 1843. BH #1908, (4:00). (2)
The Dodger. TTBB. pf. Eng. Text: American-
Folk Campaign Song. BH #1909, (1:30). (3) Simple
Gifts. TB. pf. Eng. Text: American-Folk Shak-
er. BH #1903, (1:30). (4) I Bought Me A Cat.
TBB. pf. Eng. Text: Children's Folk Song. BH
#1910, (3:00)

402 COPLAND. Old American Songs, Set II (adapted by
Copland, Wilding-White, Fine) (1) The Little
Horses (lullaby). TTBB. pf. Eng. Text: Ameri-
can Folk. BH #5510, (3:00). (2) At the River.
TTBB. pf. Eng. Text: American Folk. BH
#5514, (3:30). (3) Ching-a-ring Chaw. TTBB.
Eng. pf. Text: Minstrel-Folk Song. BH #5518,
(1:30)

403 COPLAND. Stomp Your Foot; The Tender Land. arr.
for TTBB. pf. duet. Eng. Text: Horace Everett.
BH #5136. (3:00)

404 COPLAND. Song of the Guerrillas; The North Star.
TBB. B. Solo. pf. Eng. Text: Ira Gershwin.
BH #1729. (4:00)

405 COWELL, HENRY (1897-1965). Day, Evening, Night,
Morning. TTBBB (2 part falsetto or boys' voices,
ad lib.). unac. Eng. Text: Paul Laurence Dunbar.
SOU #ME 1001. (12:00)

406 COWELL. Evening at Brookside. TTBB. T. solo.
unac. Eng. Text: Harry Cowell. SOU. #ME
1002. (4:00)

407 COWELL. Luther's Carol for His Son. TTBB. unac.
Eng. Text: James, John and Robert Wedderburn
(From Ane Compendium Buik of Godly and Spiritual
Sangis, 1567). L #L-237. (3:00)

408 COWELL. Supplication. unis. 2 tr. 2 tromb. timp.
ad lib. Eng. Text: Cowell. CFP #6322. (3:30)

409 COWELL. A Thanksgiving Psalm: from the Dead Sea
Scrolls. TTTBBB. Orch: 2 tr. B-flat, 2 hns. 2
fl. 2 ob. 2 cl. B-flat, 2 bn. timp. str. Eng. trans.
Millar Burrows. AMP, on rental

410 CRAWFORD, JOHN. Amour, Tu as été mon Maître
     (Four settings.) TTB. unac. Fr. Eng. (1) I have
     Lost All That Once I Was. (De soi-même). Text:
     Clément Marot. (2) The Fairest Maid (Je suis
     aimé de la plus belle). Text: Marot. (3) Here Is
     the God Who Looks Both Ways (Voici le Père au
     double front). Text: du Bellay. (4) All That Has
     Life and Beauty (Tout ce qui prend naissance).
     Text: du Bellay. ECS #2176, 2177, 2178, 2179

411 CRESTON, PAUL (1906-). The Celestial Vision.
     TTBB. unac. Eng. Texts: Dante, Whitman, Ar-
     juna. (Arjuna trans. Eng. Sir Edward Arnold).
     SP. (9:00)

412 CRESTON. Here Is Thy Footstool. TTBB. unac.
     Eng. Text: Tagore. GS #9793. (2:45)

413 CRESTON. Missa Adoro Te. TB. org. Lat. JF
     #8751. (18:00)

414 CRESTON. Missa Solemnis, op. 44. TTBB. (or
     SATB). org. orch. parts on rental. Lat. MM.
     (20:00)

415 CRESTON. Thou Hast Made Me Endless; Three Cho-
     rales from Tagore. TTBB. unac. Eng. Text:
     Tagore. (No. 1, SSAA; No. 3, SATB). GS #9792

416 CRESTON. Two Motets, op. 45: Adoro Te and Salve
     Regina. TTBB. org. Lat. Eng. Adoro Te: B
     solo. Text: St. Thomas Aquinas. Salve. T.
     solo. Text: attr. Hermannus Contractus. GS
     #9912. (6:00)

417 DAVIDSON, HAROLD (1908-). A Collection of Corny
     Gems. TTBB. unac. Eng. Text: Davidson. WB
     #9-3239

418 DAVIDSON. A Collection of Sad But True Ballads.
     TTBB. unac. Eng. Text: Davidson. WB #9-R3239

419 DAVIDSON. A Collection of Silly But Sad Ballads.
     TTBB. unac. Eng. Text: Davidson. WB #9-
     R3238

420 DAVIS, KATHERINE K. (1892-). The Firmament of

68   Music for Men's Voices

Power. TTBB. unac. Eng. Ps. 150, 149, 145.
WB #3797

421 DAVIS. The Humble Shepherds. TTBB. unac. Eng.
     Text: Rhys Williams. BMC #2197

422 DELANEY, ROBERT (1903-1956). Blow, Blow, Thou
     Winter Wind. TTBB. pf. Eng. Text: Shakespeare:
     As You Like It. Act II: sc. 7. ECS #2103

423 DELANEY. Full Fathom Five Thy Father Lies.
     TTBB. pf. Eng. Text: Shakespeare: Tempest,
     Act II: sc. 2. ECS #2102

424 DELLO JOIO, NORMAN (1913-). O Sing Unto the
     Lord. TBB. org. Eng. Text: Ps. 98. CF
     #7138. (4:00)

425 DIAMOND, DAVID (1915-). Let Us All Take to Sing-
     ing. TTBB. unac. Eng. Text: Herman Melville.
     SOU #ME1003

426 DIAMOND. The Martyr. TTBB. unac. Eng. Text:
     Melville. SOU #ME1004. (10:00)

427 DONATO, ANTHONY (1909-). Homesick Blues.
     TTBB. unac. Text: Langston Hughes. MMC #320

428 DONOVAN, RICHARD (1891-). Fantasy on American
     Folk Ballads. TTBB. pf. 4 hands. T. or S. solos.
     Eng. Texts: American Folk (I Pitch My Tent on
     This Campground; Farewell, my Friends; Old Ban-
     gum; Ballad of Courtship from Danville, Vermont;
     Reuben Ranzo). JF. (13:00)

429 DONOVAN. Good Ale. TTBB. unac. Eng. Text:
     John Still. CF #CM 6242. (3:30)

430 DONOVAN. I Will Sing Unto the Lord. TTBB. Bar.
     solo. org. Eng. Text: adapted from Scripture.
     AUG. (8:30)

431 FELCIANO, RICHARD. Double Alleluia. Alleluia-
     Send Forth Thy Spirit. Ps. 103:30. Alleluia--
     Come, Holy Spirit. Sequence--Come Thou Holy
     Spirit, assigned to Stephen Langton. unis. org.
     electronic tape (available from the publishers).
     Eng. WL#EEMP1532-1

432 FELCIANO. Two Hymns to Howl By. 4 ev. unac.
     Eng. Text: Allen Ginsberg. ECS #2239

433 FLOYD, CARLISLE (1926-). Death Comes Knock-
     ing. TTBB. pf. Eng. Text: Joseph Auslander.
     BH #5368

434 FRACKENPOHL, ARTHUR (1924-). Essays on Wom-
     en. TTBB. T. solo. (and short solos). pf. Eng.
     Text: Ogden Nash. CF #04698. (16:25)

435 FRACKENPOHL. Lovers Love the Spring (It Was a
     Lover and his Lass). TBB. pf. (opt. Guitar,
     drums, stb.) Eng. Text: Shakespeare; As You Like
     It. Act V: Sc. 3. EBM #110. (2:00)

436 FRACKENPOHL. Shepherds, Rejoice. TTBB. T. or
     B. solo. Brass choir: 3 hns. F. 2 tromb. Bar.
     tuba. Text: The Social Harp, Philadelphia, 1868.
     RK. (4:00)

437 FRACKENPOHL. Three Limericks in Canon Form:
     1. A Diner at Crewe. 2. A Boy of Bagdad. 3.
     A Fellow of Perth. TBB. pf. Eng. Text: Tradi-
     tional. EBM #114. (1:50; 1:30; 0:50)

438 FRIML, RUDOLF (1879-). Song of the Vagabonds;
     The Vagabond King, ed. Simeone. TTBB. pf.
     Eng. Text: Brian Hooker. SP #C140

439 FROMM, HERBERT (1905-). Stephano's Song: The
     Tempest, Act II, sc. 2. TTBB. unac. Eng. Text:
     Shakespeare. ECS #2189

440 GILL, MILTON (1932-1968). O Lord, Rebuke Me Not.
     TTBB. unac. Eng. Text: Ps. 6. SMC

441 HADLEY, HENRY (1871-1937). Night. TTBB. unac.
     Eng. Text: Washburn Harding. ROW #330. (1:00)

442 HANSON, HOWARD (1896-). Song of Democracy, op.
     44. TTBB. Eng. Text: Walt Whitman. orch.
     score reduced for pf. by Maurice Ford. CF.
     (12:00)

443 HARRIS, ROY (1898-). Mass for Male Voices and
     Organ. Lat. TTBB. CF (on rental only). (30:00)

444 HARRIS. The Working Man's Pride; Folk Fantasy for
     Festivals. TTBB. Bass-Bar. solo. speaker.
     Eng. Texts: American Folk. AMP

445 HARRISON, LOU (1917-). A Joyous Procession (1)
     and A Solemn Procession (2). H and L Voices.
     2 tromb. also in I: 4 tamborines and gong. in 2:
     8 handbells (4 players), large bass drum. Text:
     wordless. CFP #6543. (6:00)

446 HARRISON. Mass for Male and Female Voices. (all
     in unis.). tr. harp and str. Lat. (possible to do
     with men only). ACA. (28:00)

447 HEATH, FENNO (1926-). Death Be Not Proud.
     TTBB. unac. Eng. Text: John Donne. GS #11975

448 HOVHANESS, ALAN (1911-). Protest and Prayer.
     op. 41. TTBB. T. solo. org. Eng. Text: Hov-
     haness. CEP #66198. (10:00)

449 HOVHANESS. To the God Who Is in the Fire, op.
     146. TTBB. 6 perc. players (Marimba 1, Marim-
     ba II, A & E pedal timp. B. Drum, Tam-tam).
     T. solo. Eng. Text: Sh'vet Upanishad 11, 17.
     CFP #6509A. (6:00)

450 IMBRIE, ANDREW (1921-). Psalm 42. TBB. org.
     Eng. Text: Ps. 42: 1, 2, 5, 7, 8, 11. CFP
     #6888. (6:00)

451 IVES, CHARLES (1874-1954). December. Men unis.
     unac. or woodwind and brass. Eng. Text: Folgore
     da San Geminiano-Rossetti. PEER #812-2. (2:00)

452 IVES. For You and Me, ed. Clifford Richter. TTBB.
     unac. Eng. Text: unknown. JB #124. (1:00)

453 IVES. Processional: Let There Be Light. TTBBB.
     unac. Eng. Text: Rev. John Ellerton. SOU
     #ME1019. (5:00)

454 IVES. Serenity. unis. pf. Eng. Text: John G. Whit-
     tier. AMP # A 377

455 IVES. They Are There (War Song). unis. pf. Eng.
     Text: Ives. PEER #607-6. (3:00)

456 JAMES, PHILIP (1890-   ). General William Booth Enters Heaven. [Salvation Army Founder.] TTBB.
tr. C. tromb. perc. (1 player): tam-tam, B.
drum. tamb. 2 pianos (2nd interchangeable with
organ). Eng. Text: Nicholas Vachel Lindsay.
WIT. (10:00)

457 KASLTE, LEONARD (1929-   ). Three Whale Songs;
Moby Dick. TTBB. unac. T. solo. Eng. Text:
unknown. RIC #NY2246

458 KAY, ULYSSES (1917-   ). Come Away, Come Away,
Death. TBB. unac. Eng. Text: Shakespeare,
Twelfth Night. SOU # ME 1014. (3:00)

459 KAY. Triple Set. 1, Ode to the Cuckoo (TB). 2,
Had I a Heart (TB). 3, A Toast (TBB). unac.
Eng. Text: 1. Michael Bruce. 2. Richard Brinsley
Sheridan. 3. Sheridan. MCA #19519-125; 19543-
125.

460 KAY. Triumvirate: 1. Music 2. The Children's Hour
3. The Night March. TTBB. unac. Eng. Text:
(1) Ralph Waldo Emerson, (2) Henry Wadsworth
Longfellow, (3) Herman Melville. SOU #ME1013.
(12:00)

461 KEENAN, KENT (1913-   ). The Unknown Warrior
Speaks. TTBB. unac. Eng. Text: Margery Smith.
GR #5

462 KENNEDY, JOHN BRODIN (1934-   ). Little Lamb,
Who Made Thee. TB. pf. Eng. Text: William
Blake. BH #5654

463 KOHN, KARL. Three Goliard Songs: 1. Exit diluculo;
2. Stetit puella; 3. Tempus hoc letitie. TBB. unac. Lat. Text: Medieval Latin Goliard Songs. CF
#07432. (2:40; 1:25; 1:30)

464 KORTE, KARL (1928-   ). Jenny Kissed Me, (Rondeaux); Aspects of Love. TB. pf. Eng. Text:
James Henry Leigh Hunt. ECS #2114

465 KORTE. Bitter Is My Lot; Aspects of Love. TT (B)
B. unac. Eng. Text: Shao Ch'ang (Ch'ing Dynasty).
trans. Henry Hart. ECS #2310

466 KORTE. Marriage; Aspects of Love. TB.   pf. Eng.
     Text: Ralph Waldo Emerson.   ECS #211

467 KRAFT, LEO. A New Song. TBB.   unac. Eng. Text:
     Ps. 98.   MER #MC500-5

468 KUBIK, GAIL (1914-). A Sailor, He Come to Court
     Me. TTBB. unac. vn. solo. Eng. Text: Bill
     Roberts.   MMC #MC 306

469 KUBIK. Choral Profiles: Oliver De Lancey. TB.
     pf. Eng. Text: Stephen Vincent Benét.   GS #9862

470 KUBIK. Hop Up, My Ladies (American Folk Song
     Sketch). TTBB. TB solos. vn. solo. unac. Eng.
     Text: trad. with additional lyrics by Kubik.   SOU
     #24-33

471 KUBIK. John Henry (American Folk Song Sketch).
     TTBB. pf. Eng. Text: trad. American.   RIC
     #1925-14

472 KUBIK. Johnny Stiles (American Folk Song Sketch).
     TTBB. B solo. pf. Eng. Text: trad. with addi-
     tional lyrics by Kubik.   SOU #26-12

473 KUBIK. Litany and Prayer. TB (some div.) pf. re-
     duction of full score. Eng. Text. adap. by com-
     poser from Episcopal Book of Common Prayer.
     Same music, different texts: (1) A Service of Inter-
     cession for War, (2) A supplication for Deliverance
     from Sin and Guidance in the Ways of Peace.   SOU
     #ME 1011.   (12:00)

474 KUBIK. The Monotony Song (American Folk Song
     Sketch). TB. B. solo. pf. Eng. Text: Theodore
     Roethke.   RIC #1927-15

475 KURKA, ROBERT (1921-1957). Who Shall Speak for
     the People. TTBB. unac. Eng. Text: Carl Sand-
     burg.   GR #5

476 LATHAM, WILLIAM P. (1917-). Songs of a Day
     Rome Was Not Built In. TTBB. unac. Eng. Text:
     Sixth Cent. Latin Poets of Carthage, (#1 by Luxori-
     us). Eng. vers. Jack Lindsay. Four settings:
     (1) On a Hairy Philosopher, (2) A Kiss, (3) A

Boozer's Dream, (4) On a Statue of Venus. AMP
#A655

477 LOCKWOOD, NORMAND (1906-   ). Dirge for Two
Veterans. TTBB. T. solo. pf. Eng. Text: Walt
Whitman. WB #9w-3438

478 LOCKWOOD. Prelude to Western Star: Americans
and Lend Me Your Music, arr. Kunzel. TTBB.
T. solo. pf. Eng. Text: Stephen Vincent Benét.
BH #434

479 LOESSER, FRANK (1910-1970). Fugue for Tinhorns;
Guys and Dolls. TTB. pf. Eng. Text. Loesser.
FMC. (1:30)

480 LONDON, EDWIN (1927-   ). Three Settings of the
XXIII Psalm. No. 1 for TTBB. (Also settings for
female and mixed voices). unac. Lat. MJQ

481 MOE, DANIEL. I Will Extol Thee. TTBB. unac.
Eng. Text: Ps. 145. AUG #Ps. 623

482 MOEVS, ROBERT (1920-   ). Cantata Sacra. TTBB.
Bar. solo. fl. 3 tromb. timp. (2 picc., 1 grande
autom). Lat. In 4 Mvts: (1) Introit, 4th Sun.
after Easter, Cantate Domino, Ps. 97: 1-2.   (2)
Alleluia, 4th Sunday after Easter, Dextera Dei,
Ps. 117:16.   (3) Offertory, Easter Sun., Terra
tremuit, Ps. 75: 9, 10.   (4) Communion, 5th Sun.
after Easter, Cantate Domino, Ps. 95:2. ACL

483 MOORE, DOUGLAS (1893-1970).   Simon Legree.
TTBB. Bar. solo. pf. Eng. Text: Vachel Lindsay.
CF #CM2230

484 NELSON, RON (1929-   ). Behold Man. TTBB. unac.
Eng. Text: Albert van Nostrand. BH #5403

485 NELSON. Meditation on the Syllable OM. TTBB.
T. B. solos. unac. Eng. Text: James Schevill.
BH #5809. (6:18)

486 NORDEN, HUGO (1909-   ). O Satisfy Us With Thy
Mercy. TTBB. unac. Eng. Text: from Ps. 90.
ABIN #APM-406

487   NOSS, LUTHER (1907-). Psalms and Hymns of
      Early America, in 3 Vol. I: Two Tunes from the
      Ainsworth Psalter. (1) By Babels River, Ps. 137.
      (2) O Praise Jah, Ps. 150. Vol. II: Three Tunes
      from the Bay Psalm Book. (1) Harken, O God, Ps.
      61: 1-4, 8. (2) O God, to Rescue Mee, Ps. 70.
      (3) Yee Heav'ns of Heav'ns, Ps. 148: 1-9. Vol. III:
      Two Tunes from The Missouri Harmony. (1)
      Through Ev'ry Age, Ps. 90, paraphrased by Isaac
      Watts. (2) Glorious Things of Thee, by John New-
      ton. All for TBB. unac. AMP #A225, A226,
      A227

488   NOWAK, LIONEL. Wisdom Exalteth Her Children.
      TBB-TBB. unac. Eng. Text: Ecclesiastes 4:
      11-12. ALB #BC52. (3:15)

489   PERSICHETTI, VINCENT (1915-). Four Cummings
      Choruses, op. 98. TB. pf. Eng. Text: E. E.
      Cummings. #1222 Dominic Has a Doll; #1223
      Nouns to Nouns; #1224 Maggie and Milly and Molly
      and May; #1225 Uncles. EVC. (6:00 Tot.)

490   PERSISCHETTI. Jimmie's Got a Goil. TB. pf. 4
      hands. Text: E. E. Cummings. GS #9800.
      (3:00)

491   PERSICHETTI. Sam Was a Man. TB. pf. Eng.
      Text: E. E. Cummings. GS #9791. (3:00)

492   PERSICHETTI. Song of Peace. TTBB. pf. (org.)
      Eng. Text: Anon. EVC #130. (3:00)

493   PINKHAM, DANIEL (1923-). Mass of the Good
      Shepherd. unis. org. Eng. IONE

494   PINKHAM. Te Deum. TB (SA). 3 tr. B-flat, org.
      Eng. trans. John Dryden. RK #613 (4:30)

495   PISK, PAUL (1893-). Psalm XXX. TTBB. unac.
      Eng. SOU # ME 1012

496   PISTON, WALTER (1894-). Carnival Song. TBB.
      pf. 4 hands or Brass: 3 tr. C, 3 hns. F, 3 tromb.
      tuba. It. Text: DeMedici. ARP #A296. (8:00)

497   QUILTER, ROGER (1877-1953). Non nobis Domine.

TB. pf. Eng. Text: Rudyard Kipling. BH # MFS
348

498 REVICKI, ROBERT. Songs of Praise: Dominus illu-
minatis mea and Alleluia. 2 ev. unac. tamborine,
triangle, cymbals (2 players). BH # 5597. (2:15;
1:15)

499 RIEGGER, WALLINGFORD (1885-1951). Evil Shall
Not Prevail. TBB-TBB. unac. Eng. Text: Wisdom 7:29-30. ALB # BCS3. (6:50)

500 ROGERS, BERNARD (1892-1968). Psalm 18. TTBB.
T. solo. pf. Eng. TP # 312-40600

501 ROREM, NED (1923-). A Sermon on Miracles.
solo voice, unis. chorus and strings: vn. 1 and 2,
va. vc. stb. (keyboard). "The work should be sung
either by a male choir with a female soloist or
female choir with a male soloist. " Eng. Text:
Paul Goodman. BH. (6:00)

502 ROREM. I Feel Death. TBB. unac. Eng. Text:
John Dryden. BH # 5624. (1:00)

503 ROREM. Proper, Votive Mass of the Holy Spirit.
unis. org. Eng. Text: Ps. 103: 30 and Stephen
Langton. BH # 5618. (9:00)

504 SCHUMAN, WILLIAM (1910-). Attention, Ladies
(from Mail Order Madrigals). TBB. unac. Eng.
Text: freely adapted from the Sears, Roebuck 1897
catalog. TP # 342-40029

505 SCHUMAN. Deo ac veritati. TTB. unac. Lat. Text:
trad. Lat. Motto of Colgate University. TP # 342-
40015

506 SCHUMAN. Four Rounds on Famous Words: Health;
Thrift; Caution; Beauty. TTBB. (SATB). unac.
Eng. Text: trad. TP # 342-4000, 1, 2, 3. (0:30;
1:30; 1:00; 2:15)

507 SCHUMAN. Holiday Song. TTBB. pf. Eng. Text:
Genevieve Taggard. GS # 9866. (2:30)

508 SCHUMAN. Truth Shall Deliver. TBB. unac. Eng.

Text: adap. Marion Farquhar from Chaucer. GS
#9597. (4:00)

509 SESSIONS, ROGER (1895-). Mass for Unison Choir
and Organ. Eng. EBM #77. (15:00)

510 SOWERBY, LEO (1895-1969). A Liturgy of Hope.
TTBB. S. solo. org. Eng. Text: Ps. 80. BMC
#8065

511 SOWERBY. Psalm 70. TTBB. org. Eng. GR #2982

512 SOWERBY. Psalm 124. TTBB. org. Eng. GR
#1986

513 SOWERBY. Psalm 133. TTBB. org. Eng. GR
#2982

514 STARER, ROBERT (1924-). Never Seek to Tell Thy
Love. TTBB. unac. Eng. Text: William Blake.
SOU #ME1023

515 STERNE, COLIN. Three Anthems for Easter. TB.
unison congregation. org. Eng. 1. Crave as New-
born Babes. Text: Petr. I: 2, 2 and Ps. 80: 1-5,
9-10, 12-17. 2. An Angel of the Lord. Text:
Matt. 28: 2, 5, 6, and Ps. 117: 1-3, 5-9. 3.
Put in Your Hand. Text: John 20:27. WL.
#EMP--1595-2

516 SURINACH, CARLOS. The Mission of San Antonio: A
Symphonic Canticle in five parts. TB (difficult to
extract as solos. Vocal parts part of symphonic
fabric). Orch: 3 fl. (picc.), 3 ob. (Eng. Hn.), 3
cl. B-flat (B. cl), 2 bn. contra bn. 4 hns. F, 3
tr. C, 3 tromb. tuba, timp. 3 perc. players.
Celesta, Harp, str. Lat. (1) Espada--Hallowed
Trophy, Text: trad. in honor of St. Francis of
Assisi. (2) San Juan--Song of Fauna. (3) Concep-
ción--Holy Womb. Text: section from Credo of
the Mass, et incarnatus est--. (4) El Alamo--
Epitaph. (5) San Jose--Celebration. Text: Tantum
Ergo. AMP. (22:00)

517 SWANSON, HOWARD (1909-). Nightingales. TTBB.
(some div.) T. B. solos. unac. Eng. Text: Robert
Bridges. MSC

518 THOMPSON, RANDALL (1899-   ). The Gate of Heaven.
     TTBB. unac. Eng. Text: Ps. 122: 1; Habakkuk
     2:20; Genesis 28: 17. ECS #2175

519 THOMPSON. The Last Words of David. TTBB. pf.
     Eng. Text: II Samuel 23: 3, 4. ECS #2154.
     (5:00)

520 THOMPSON. The Pasture; Frostiana. TBB. pf.
     Eng. Text: R. Frost. ECS #2181-2. (2:15)

521 THOMPSON. Quis multa gracilis; Six Odes of Horace.
     TBB. unac. Lat. Text: Horace, Odes 1, 5.
     ECS #739

522 THOMPSON. Stopping by Woods on a Snowy Evening;
     Frostiana. TTBB. pf. Eng. Text: R. Frost.
     ECS #2181-6. (3:30)

523 THOMPSON. Tarantella. TTBB. pf. Eng. Text:
     Hilaire Belloc. ECS #560. (6:00)

524 THOMPSON. The Testament of Freedom. TTBB.
     pf. Eng. Text: Thomas Jefferson. ECS #2118.
     (25:00)

525 THOMSON, VIRGIL (1896-   ). Capital Capitals.
     BBBB (TTBB). pf. Eng. Text: Gertrude Stein.
     Possible by solo quartet. (Capital Capitals by
     Gertrude Stein, 1923, evokes Provence, its land-
     scapes, food and people, as a conversation among
     the cities Aix, Arles, Avignon and Les Baux, here
     called capitals One, Two, Three and Four. It also
     reflects the poet's attachment to that sunny region,
     which she had first known as an ambulance driver
     in WW I). BH #554. (11:00)

526 THOMSON. Mass for Solo Voice and Unis. Choir.
     pf. Lat. GS #2473

527 THOMSON. Mass for Two Part Chorus. unac. perc.
     player, (ad lib.). Lat. Eng. L. (14:00)

528 THOMSON. Missa pro Defunctis; Sanctus. TTBB.
     pf. Lat. GR

529 THOMSON. Agnus Dei. 3 ev. unac. Lat. Text: Mass
     text. MMC. (2:10)

530 TITCOMB, EVERETT (1884-). Magnificat. 3 ev.
     org. Eng. Text: Luke I: 46-56. BMC #12333

531 TITCOMB. Behold Now, Praise the Lord. TTBB.
     pf. Eng. Text: adap. Ps. 134. MM#64158

532 TITCOMB. Missa Sancti Joannis Evangelistae. TTBB.
     unac. Eng. Text: Mass. CF #CM 444

533 TITCOMB. The Spirit of the Lord. TTBB. unac.
     Eng. Text: Luke 4: 18-19. ABIN #APM 207

534 WAGNER, JOSEPH (1900-). David Jazz. TTBB.
     pf. Eng. Text: Edwin Meade Robinson. ROW #259

535 WASHBURN, ROBERT (1929-). Three Shakespearean
     Folk Songs. TTBB. hnF. pf. Eng. Text: Shake-
     speare. 1. O Mistress Mine; Twelfth Night. II:3.
     2. Come Away, Death; Twelfth Night, 11:4. 3.
     Sigh No More Ladies; Much Ado About Nothing.
     II:3. OX#95-109. (9:30 Tot.)

536 WIENHORST, RICHARD (1920-). Seven Contemporary
     Chorale Settings for Voices. T(T)BB. unac. Eng.
     Texts: Various hymn texts. CON #98-1130

537 WUORINEN, CHARLES (1938-). Madrigale Spirituale.
     TB. 2 ob., vn. 1 and 2 vc. pf. Lat. Text: Ps.
     2: 1-4. ACA

COLLECTIONS OF MUSIC

by composer; mainly Renaissance collections;
all periods; rounds; liturgical; college

ORLANDO DI LASSO. Cantiones duorum vocum
(Magnum opus I-XX), ed. Boepple. 12 Motets for 2 Voices.
unac. Lat. MP. (1) Beatus vir (Ecclesiastes 14:22), (2)
Beatus homo (Proverbs 3:13, 14), (3) Oculos non irdit
(Corinthians II:9), (4) Justus cor suum tradit (Ecclesiastes
39:6), (5) Expectatio justorum (Proverbs 10:28, 29), (6)
Qui sequitur me (John 8:12), (7) Justi tulerunt spolia (Wis-
dom 10:10, 20), (8) Sancti mei venire (Matthew 16:24), (9)
Qui vult venire (Matthew 16:24), (10) Serve bone (Matthew
25:23), (11) Fulgebant justi (Old Breviary), (12) Sicut rosa
(Old Breviary).

FRANZ LISZT. Original music for male voices.
(1) Cantico del sol di San Francisco d'Assisi, unis., B.
solo., org., and orch.; (2) Mass; (3) Requiem; (4) Te Deum
(men's version); (5) Psalm 18, male chorus, orch.; (6)
Psalm 116, male chorus, piano; (7) Psalm 129, male chorus,
B. solo, organ. From the Collected Works, ed. Busoni,
Bartók, Raabe, de Motte. Available from Gregg, c/o JB.

FRANZ SCHUBERT. Complete works for men's
voices. 4 study scores (volumes). KAL. #1060, 1061,
1062, 1097. Vol. I (#1060): (1) Nachtgesang im Walde
(Sei uns stets gegrüsst, O Nacht), op. 139b. TTBB. 4
hnsE. Ger. Text: J. G. Seidl. (2) Hymne (Herr, Unser
Gott), op. 154. TTBB-TTBB. 2 ob. 2 cl. C, 2 bn. 2 tr.
C, 2 hn. 3 tromb. Ger. Text: Schmidl. (3) Gesang der
Geister über den Wassern (Des Menschen Seele gleicht dem
Wasser), op. 167 (1821 version). TTTT-BBBB. va. I and
II, vc. I and II, stb. Ger. Text: Goethe. (4) Das Dörfchen
(Ich rühme mir mein Dörfchen hier), op. 11, no. 1. TTBB.
guitar or pf. Ger. Text: Bürger. (5) Die Nachtigall (Bes-
cheiden verborgen im buschichten Gang), op. 11, no. 2.
TTBB. guitar or pf. Ger. Text: Ungar. (6) Geist der

Liebe (Der Abend schleirt Flur und Hain), op. 11, no. 3.
TTTBB. guitar or pf. Ger. Text: Matthisson. (7) Frühlingsgesang (Schmücket die Locken), op. 16, no. 1. TTBB.
guitar or pf. Ger. Text: Von Schober. (8) Naturgenuss
(Im Abendschimmer wallt der Quell), op. 16, no. 2. TTBB.
guitar or pf. Ger. Text: Matthisson.

SCHUBERT. Vol. II (#1061): (9) Der Gonderfahrer
(Es tanzen Mond und Sterne), op. 28. TTBB. pf. Ger.
Text: J. Mayhofer. (10) Bootgesang, op. 52, no. 3.
TTBB. pf. Ger. Text: from Walter Scott "Fraulein vom
See," trans. Adam Strock. (11) Zur Guten Nacht (Horcht
auf), op. 81, no. 3. TTBB. Bar. solo. pf. Ger. Text:
Rochlitz. (12) Widerspruch (Wenn ich durch Busch und
Zweig), op. 105, no. 1. TTBB. pf. Ger. Text: J. G.
Seidl. (13) Nachtelle (Die Nacht ist heiter), op. 134.
TTBB. T solo. pf. Ger. Text: J. G. Seidl. (14) Ständ-
chen (Zögernd, leise), op. 135. TTBB. A solo. pf. Ger.
Text: Franz Grillparzer. (15) Im Gegenwärtigen Vergan-
genes (Ros' and Lilie). TTBB. pf. Ger. Text: Goethe.
(16) Trinklied (Freunde, sammelt Euch). TTBB. B solo.
pf. Ger. Text: unknown. (17) Trinklied (Auf! Jeder sei).
TTBB. pf. Ger. Text: unknown. (18) Bergknappenlied
(Hinab, ihr Bruder). TTBB. pf. Ger. Text: unknown.
(19) La Pastorella. TTBB. pf. It. Text: Goldoni. (20-
23) Vier Gesänge, op. 17. TTBB. unac. Ger.: (A) Jüng-
lingswonne--Text: Matthison; (B) Liebe--Text: Schiller;
(C) Zum Rundetanz--Text: Salis; (D) Die Nacht--Text: unknown. (24-26) Drei Gesänge, op. 64. TTBB. unac. Ger.
(A) Wehmuth--Text: H. Huttenbrenner; (B) Ewige Liebe--
Text: E. Schulze; (C) Flucht--Text: C. Lappe. (27) Mon-
denschein (Des Mondes Zauber), op. 102. TTBB. T solo.
unac. Ger. Text: Fr. Von Schober. (28) Schlachtlied
(Mit Unserm Arm), op. 151. TTBB-TTBB. unac. Ger.
Text: Von Klopstock. (29) Trinklied (Edit, Nonna), op.
155. TTBB. a cap. Ger. Text: from the XIV Cent.
Rittgraff's Historische Antiquitaten. (30) Nachtmusik (Wir
Stimmen), op. 156. TTBB. unac. Ger. Text: Sigmund
von Seckendorf.

SCHUBERT. Vol. III (#1062): (31) Frühlingsgesang
(Schmücket die Locken). TTBB. unac. Ger. Text: Fr.
Von Schober. (32) Der Geistertanz (Die Bretterne Kammer).
TTBB. unac. Ger. Text: Matthisson. (33) Gesang der
Geister über den Wassern (Des Menschen Seele), 1817 ver-
sion. TTBB. unac. Ger. Text: Goethe. (34) Lied im
Freien (Wie schön ist's). TTBB. Ger. Text: J. G.

Salis. (35) Sehnsucht (Nur wer die Sehnsucht). TTBBB.
unac. Ger. Text: Goethe. (36) Ruhe, Schönstes Glück der
Erde. TTBB. unac. Ger. Text: unknown. (37) Wein
und Liebe (Liebchen und der Saft). TTBB. unac. Ger.
Text: Haug. (38) Der Entfernten (Wohl denk'ich). TTBB.
unac. Ger. Text: Salis. (39) Die Einsiedelei (Es rieselt).
TTBB. unac. Ger. Text: Salis. (40) An den Frühling
(Willkommen Schöner Jüngling). TTBB. unac. Ger. Text:
Schiller. (41) Grab und Mond (Silber blauer). TTBB.
unac. Ger. Text: Seidl. (42) Hymne (Komm, Heil'ger
Geist). TTBB-TTBB solos. unac. Ger. Text: A. Schmidl.
(43) Wer ist gross. TTBB. 2 ob., 2 bn., 2 hn. F, 2
tr. F, timp. F, str. Ger. Text: unknown. (44) Beitrag
(Birthday Song to Salieri). Ger.: (A) TTBB. unac.; (B)
TTBB. T. solo. pf.; (C) Canon a tre. (45) Gesang der
Geister über den Wassern (1820 version). TTTT-BBBB.
2 va. 2 vc. stb. Ger. Text: Goethe. (46) Das Dörfchen
(Ich ruhme mir). TTBB. unac. Ger. Text: Burger.

SCHUBERT. Vol. IV (#1097): (47) Gesang der
Geister über den Wassern (1820 version). TTBB. pf.
Ger. Text: Goethe. (48) Fischerlied (Das Fischer gewer-
be). TTBB. unac. Ger. Text: Salis. (49) Frühlingslied
(Geöffnet sind des Winters Riegel). TTBB. unac. Ger.
Text: A. Pollak. (50) Terzette. TTB. unac. Ger. Text:
Schiller. (A) Unendliche Freude; (B) Hier strecket; (C) Ein
jugendlicher Maienschwung; (D) Thronend; (E) Majestät'sche
Sonnerossa; (F) Frisch athmet; (G) Dreifach ist der Schritt.

Also, in the complete works of Schubert (Breitkopf
und Härtel) the following four are for men's voices: (1)
Salve Regina. TTBB. a cap. Lat. Text: Rosamunde
(Schauspiele). Geistchor (In der Tiefe wohnt das licht).
TTBB. 2 hns. D, tromb.: A. T. B. Ger. Text: Von
Chezy. (2) Alfonso und Estrella (opera). choruses for
TTBB. Ger. pf. (orch.). Text: Von Schober. Act II:
(A) Stille, Freunde, seht euch. B. solo; (B) Wo ist sie,
was kommt ihr zu kunden. Bar. solo; (C) Die Prinzessin
ist erschienen. S. Bar. solos; (D) Darf mich dein Kind
urnarmen. S. Bar. solos. Act III: (A) Welche Stimme.
S. T. B. solos; (B) Wehe, Wehe! Meine Vaters Scharen
sch'ich. S. T. solos; (C) Sie haben das Rufen vernommen.
T. solo. (3) Claudin Von Villa Bella. Was geht her vor.
S. T. Bar. solos, (singspiel). 2 choruses for TTBB.
Ger. pf. (orch.) Text: Goethe. (A) Rauberlied (Mit Mädchen sich vertragen). T solo; (B) Finale--Deinen Willen
nachzugeben. T. B. solos. (4) Die Bürgschaft (opera).

Quartet: Hinter Buschen, hinterm. Lamb. TTBB. a cap.
Ger. Adrast (opera). TTBB. pf. (orch.) Ger. Text: Joh.
Mayrhofer. (A) Introduction: Dank dir Gotten. T. solo;
(B) Chorus and Ensemble: Dem König Heil. Bar solo.

Anthems for Men's Voices, Vol. II for Tenors and
Basses, ed. le Huray, Temperley, Tranchell, Willcocks.
OX. Anthems in their original languages and in transla-
tion, from the period ca. 1450 to ca. 1800. Listed alpha-
betically by composer: (1) Anon. (ca. 1560). If Ye Be
Risen Again. TTBB. unac. Eng. Text: Col. 3: 1, 2.
(2) Byrd, William. Jesu nostra redemptio. TTBB. unac.
Lat. Text: Hymn, Compline, Ascension. (3) Dunstable,
John. Veni sancte spiritus. TBB. unac. Lat. Text:
Whitsunday Sequence, assigned to Stephen Langton. (4)
Ferrabosco II, Alphonso. Fuerunt mihi lacrime. TTBB.
org. Lat. Text: Ps. 42:3. (5) Handl, Jacob. De caelo
veniet. TTBB. unac. Lat. Text: unknown. (6) Locke,
Matthew. Lord Rebuke Me Not. TTB. (TBB). org. Eng.
Text: Ps. 6:1-4. (7) Marcello, Benedetto. Thy Mercy
Jehovah. TTB. org. Eng. Text: Ps. 36: 7-9, para-
phrased, J. Garth. (8) Marcello. To Thee, O Lord, My
God. TB. org. Eng. Text: Ps. 25: 1, paraphrased, J.
Garth. (9) Palestrina, Giovanni. Ecce nunc benedicta.
TTBB (BBBB). unac. Lat. Text: Ps. 134: 1-4. (10)
Palestrina. O vos omnes. TTBB. unac. Lat. Text:
Lam. I:12. (11) Praetorius, Michael. A Safe Stronghold.
TTB (TBB). unac. Eng. Text: Luther, based on Ps. 46.
(12) Praetorius. O God, From Heaven Look Below.
TTBB. unac. Eng. Text: Luther, based on Ps. 12. (13)
Purcell, Henry. Let the Words of My Mouth. TTB. org.
Eng. Text: Ps. 19:14. (14) Purcell. Since God So Tender
a Regard. TTB. org. Eng. Text: Ps. 116. (15) Schütz,
Heinrich. Jubilate Deo in chordis. TTB. org. Eng. Lat.
Text: Ps. 150:4; Ps. 87:4. (16) Shepherd, John. Christ
Rising Again. TTBB. unac. Eng. Text: Book of Common
Prayer, 1549. (17) Tomkins, Thomas. My Voice Shalt
Thou Hear. TTBB. unac. Eng. Text: Ps. 51:1. (18)
Tomkins. Have Mercy Upon Me, O Lord. TBB. unac.
Eng. Text: Ps. 5:3. (19) Vittoria, Tomas. O Regina
Caeli. TTBB. unac. Lat. Text: Matins, Sunday after
Christmas Day.

Medieval and Renaissance Choral Music, ed. Georgia
Stevens. ev. unac. MCR

Sacred Chorus, Collection by Old Masters. Vol. IV

for equal voices.   unac. Lat.   KAL.   Vol. IV: (1) O felix
anima, Carissimi, 3 ev.; (2) Confitemini Domino, Costantini, 3 ev.; (3) Benedicam Dominum in omne tempore,
Croce, 4 ev.; (4) Exaudi Deus, Croce, 3 ev.; (5) Christus
factus est, Handl, 4 ev.; (6) De caelo veniet, Handl, 3 ev.;
(7) Adoramus te, Lassus, 3 ev.; (8) Hodie apparuit in
israel, Lassus, 3 ev.; (9) Verbum caro, Lassus, 3 ev.;
(10) Vere languores nostros, Lotti, 3 ev.; (11) In monte
oliveti, Martini, 3 ev.; (12) O salutaris hostia, Martini, 3
ev.; (13) Tristis est anima mea, Martini, 3 ev.; (14) Jesu,
salvator mundi, Menegali, 3 ev.; (15) Laetamini in Domino,
Nanini, 3 ev.; (16) Christe lux vera, Palestrina, 4 ev.;
(17) Confitemini Domino, Palestrina, 4 ev.; (18) Salve
Regina, Palestrina, 4 ev.; (19) Sub tuum, Palestrina, 4
ev.; (20) O salutaris, Pierre de la Rue, 4 ev.; (21) O
salutaris, Pisari, 3 ev.; (22) Adoramus te, Pitoni, 4 ev.;
(23) Adoramus te, Ruffo, 4 ev.; (24) Laudate Dominum,
Viadana, 4 ev.; (25) Monstra te esse matrem, Vittoria, 3
ev.; (26) O sacrum convivium, Vittoria, 4 ev.

Secunda Anthologia Vocalis, comp. and ed. O. Ra-
vanello. Motets for 3 ev. including Anerio, Isaak, Lassus,
Lotti, Nanini, Palestrina, Pitoni, Praetorius, Tartini,
Vittoria.   MCR #1188

Ten Glees, ed. Marshall Bartholomew. (Madrigals
and Airs). 3 ev. MP

Vade Mecum, collection of motets, hymns, offer-
tories for four male voices. unac. Vol. II, comp. J. B.
Hoffman, JF #3485; Vol. III, comp. J. B. Hoffman, JF
#5275. Of particular interest: Vol. II: (1) Isaak: O esca
viatorum; (2) Nanini: Hodie Christus natus est; (3) Pales-
tina: Pie Jesu; Vol. III: (1) Anerio: Christus factus est;
(2) Casciolini: Panis angelicus; (3) Casciolini: Tenebrae
factae sunt; (4) Lotti: Regina caeli; (5) Palestrina: Tantum
ergo; (6) Roselli: Adoramus te, Christe; (7) Vittoria:
Popule meus.

One of the most useful collections of choral music
for men's voices is the Harvard University Glee Club Collection, in 6 vols., Archibald T. Davison, ed. ECS #50,
100, 1000, 1050, 1100, 1400. Although not all are original
works for men's voices, the quality of music and editorial
scholarship made this a pioneer collection of great insight.
Many of the individual pieces are published separately by
E. C. Schirmer. The earliest composers are from the

Renaissance.   There are 32 sacred works by Anerio, Byrd,
des Prez, Gabrieli, Hassler, Lassus, Morales, Praetorius,
Schütz, Sweelinck, Viadana, Vittoria; and 16 secular pieces,
including madrigals by Dowland, Lassus, Marenzio, Monteverdi, Morley, Weelkes, Wilbye.   In addition to 11 arrangements by J. S. Bach and 7 by Handel, the collection includes Carissimi, Durante, Lotti, Pergolesi, Purcell from
the Baroque.   Although Mozart and Haydn are not included,
Davison does include Gretry and Gluck who could be considered part of the classical school.   Beethoven is represented by 2 works.   The Romantic period together with composers of the Russian liturgical tradition is represented by
15 compositions.   In addition, 4 operatic excerpts and 13
Gilbert and Sullivan are part of the collection.   Finally, over
34 arrangements of both familiar and non-familiar carols and
folk songs round out the survey.

Fifteen Anonymous Elizabethan Rounds (from a parch-
ment roll in the library of King's College, Cambridge), ed.
Jill Vlasto and William Tortolano.   SB #5356.

Nineteen Liturgical Rounds, ed. Tortolano.   GI #G-
1600.

Anthems for Unison Choir.   pf. GS #2660 (45 arrangements and original works).

A Short Mass in Canonic Style, with Rounds, Canons
and Alleluias, ed. Tortolano.   MCR #2870

Five Centuries of Alleluias and Amens, comp. Hawley
Ades.   Shawneee Press.   In 3 Vols.   Men's voices: Vol.
I: Van Kerle: Amen; Asola: Amen; Hassler: Amen.   Vol.
II: Liszt: Amen.

Friday Evening Melodies, arr. Israel Goldfarb.   Unis.
and 2 part.   Hebrew Synagogue music.   BLOCH.

The Harvard Song Book, comp. and ed. Elliot Frobes.
ECS #628.   (85 songs of Harvard, other colleges, traditional songs of the Harvard Glee Club and motets).   Most of
these arrangements are available in Octavo from ECS.

Songs of Yale, comp. and ed. Marshall Bartholomew.
GS #1516.

CATALOGS OF FOREIGN PUBLISHERS

The reader is highly encouraged to explore the excellent editions available from the catalogs of foreign publishers. The selections from the following catalogs are of particular interest.

CATALOG from ANNIE BANK, Anna Vondelstraat 13, Amsterdam, Holland (American representative--WL).

Masses

Anon. ca. 1540
  Missa 3 ev. TTB. unac. Lat. #JA 14
Anon. ca. 1500
  Missa In Honorem Beatae Maria Virgine.
  TTBB. unac. Lat. # bru 2
Asola, Giovanni
  Missa Sexti Toni. TTBB. unac. Lat. #JA1
Casciolini, C. O., 1775-1844
  Missa Sine Nomine. TTB. unac. Lat. #JC 5
Jachetus, ca. 1550
  Missa O Quam Pulchra. TTBB. unac. Lat. # bru 6
Palestrina, Giovanni
  Missa Aeterna Christi Munera. TTBB. unac.
  Lat. # JP 6
  Missa Sine Nomine. TTBB. unac. Lat. #JP9
Ruffo, Vincenzo
  Missa Alma Redemptoris. TTBB. unac. Lat. # bru 8
Sermisy, Claudin de
  Missa Tota Pulchra Es. TTBB. unac. Lat. # JS 6
Tallis, Thomas
  Missa 4 ev. TTBB. unac. Lat. # JT 2

Motets and Madrigals

(all TTBB. unac. Lat. unless indicated otherwise) catalog numbers and text sources not given.

Agostini, Paolo (died 1629): Adoramus Te: O bone Jesu; O sacrum convivium; Panis angelicus.

Aichinger, Gregor: Adoramus te.

Asola, Giovanni: Adoramus te; Ave rex noster, TTB; Cantate Domino, TTB; Passio sec. joannem; Omnes de saba; O vos omnes, TTB; Quem vidistis; Tantum ergo.

Brumel, Antone: O Domine Jesu.

Carissimi, Giacomo (1605-1674): Tantum ergo, TTB.

Casciolini: Sacris solemniis.

Costantini, Alessandro (late 16th Cent.): Confitemini Domino, TTB.

Croce, Giovanni: Cantate Domino; O vos omnes; Tenebrae; Virtute magna.

Festa, Costanzo (died 1545): All TTB. Ave Regina; O pulcherrima; Quam pulchra es; Sancta Maria; Surge amica; Veni creator.

Franck, Melchior (1573-1639): O Domine Jesu.

Gombert, Nicolas (died 1556): Virgo S. Catharina.

Handl, Jacob: Ascendit Deus; Ave Maria; Beata es; Canite tuba; Dicunt infantes; Ecce Quomodo; Gloria laus; Haec dies, TTBB-TTBB; In nomine Jesu; Natus est nobis; O beata trinitas (TTBB-TTBB); O magnum mysterium (TTBB-TTBB); O sacrum convivium; Pueri concinite; Pueri hebraeorum; Surrexit pastor; Ad adjuvandum, TTB.

Ingegneri, Marcantonio (1545-1592): Ecce enim evangelizo; O bone Jesu; Virgo prudentissima; O Domine Jesu.

Isaac, Heinrich (1450-1517): Innsbruck, ich muss dich lassen, TTTT. Ger.

Lassus, Orlandus: Adoramus, TTB; Agimus tibi gratias, TTB; Alleluia, laus et gloria; Ave Maria, alta stirps; Convertere; Die Welt; Herr, der du m. Stärke; TTB; Hodie apparuit, TTB; In pace in idipsum, TTB; O bone Jesu, TTB; O Herr, ich Klag, TTB; Tantum ergo; Tibi laus; Verbo caro, TTT; Tantum ergo, TTT; Wie ein Hirsch, TTTB.

Martini, Giambattista: Adoramus te; In monte oliveti; O salutaris hostia; Tristis est anima (all TTB).

Monteverdi, Claudio: Ave Maria, TTB; Crucifixus; O Domine Jesu Christe, TTB; Surgens Jesus, TTB.

Nanino, Giovanni: Laetamini in Domino, TTB.

Obrecht, Jacob (1450-1505): La tortorella; Parce Domine, TBB.

Palestrina, Giovanni: Ave Maris Stella, TBB; Confitimini; Hodie Christus natus est; Innocentes: Jesu rex admirabile, TTB; Lectio III (in Coena Dom.), TTTBB; Exultate Deo; Lectio III (feria VI in Paresceve), TTTBB; Lectio III (In Sabbato Sancto); Ave Regina; Salve Regina;

O crux ave; Popule meus; Pueri hebraeorum; Sub tuum praesidium; Surrexit pastor; Tantum ergo, TTBBB.

Pitoni, Giuseppe (1657-1743): Tantum ergo.

Porta, Costanzo (1530-1601): Dies sanctificatus; O sacrum convivium; Regina Coeli; Salve Regina.

des Prez, Josquin: O Domine Jesu.

de Rore, Cipriano (1516-1665): Hic est panis; O crux benedicta; Sub tuum praesidium. de la Rue, Pierre, (-1518) O salutaris.

Sweelinck, Jan (1562-1621): Vous pouvez, TTB. Fr.; Yeux, qui quidez, TTB, Fr.

Viadana, Ludovico da (1564-1627): Ave verum; O sacrum convivium; O salutaris hostia, TTB.

Vittoria, Tomas: Aestimatus sum; Ave Maris Stella, TBB; Due seraphim; Natus est nobis, O regem coeli; O sacrum convivium; Tenebrae; Una hora; Verbo caro/Tantum ergo, TBB; Domine, non sum dignus.

Willaert, Adrian (1480/90-1572): Ave virginum gemma; In quacumque die, TTB; O Domine Jesu.

Selected list of music for men's voices from the CATALOG OF GALAXY, agents for Stainer and Bell, Ltd., of London. Of particular interest are the following titles of English secular music, madrigals and part songs from the Renaissance. Part I (all TBB, unac., Eng., catalog numbers and text sources not available): (1) John Wilbye (1574-1638): Away, Thou Shalt not Love Me; Ay Me Can Every Rumour; Dear Pity How. (2) Thomas Weelkes: Come, Sirrah Hack Ho; This World Doth Pass; Since Robin Hood. (3) Thomas Morley: Cruel, You Pull Away Too Soon; Lady, Those Eyes; The Nightingale; O Sleep Fond Fancy. Part II (all TTBB, unac. Eng., catalog numbers and text sources not available): (1) John Bennet (ca. 1570-1614?): Cruel Unkind; Lure Falconers; Sing Out Ye Nymphs. (2) Thomas Morley: Hark, Jolly Shepherds; Ho, Who Comes Here; Lady, Why Grieve You Still Me. (3) Thomas Weelkes: Lo, Country Sports. (4) John Word: O My Thoughts; Satyr Once Did Run Away.

Selected list of music for men's voices from the CATALOG OF B. SCHOTTS SOHNE, Mainz, Germany. Of particular interest are the following titles by 20th-century German composers: (1) Werner Egk (1901-   ): Die Entschlafenen; Glaubenslied; Lied der Welt. (2) Paul Hindemith: Die Stiefmutter; Nun da der Tag. (3) Carl Orff: Sonnengesang der heiligen Franziskus; Zwei dreistimmige Chorsätze; Zwei Geistliche Chorsätze. (4) Ernst Pepping (1901-): Mitten wir im Leben.

INDEX OF AUTHORS AND SOURCES OF TEXTS

The index includes the following information: (1) The name of the author, translator, Biblical reference, national origin, Mass text, liturgical day, or sacred book. If the text source is not certain, it is listed as anonymous or unknown. With the former, one can generally ascertain at least the century or national origin. (2) The dates of the author or translator, if available. (3) If an author is used more than once by the same composer, this is indicated in parentheses (e.g., Claudel (2)--Milhaud). (4) In certain cases, the literary source is given. This is particularly the case in Shakespeare's plays. (5) The composer's name. (6) And finally, a number or numbers referring to the entry in the Individual Composers section.

89

INDEX OF FIRST LINES AND TITLES

The index includes the following information: (1) The title of the composition in its original language; its translation, if included in the music; the source, in particular opera, oratorio, cantata, choral cycle. If the first line of a composition is different from the title, this is usually listed. (2) The composer.